The Broken Spoke

Mike Wesolowski

ISBN: 979-8-3303-4054-5

Disclaimer: Throughout this book the author talks about experiences and the treatments he has undergone to help himself heal. The author is not a medical or psychological professional. Please consult with your doctor or therapist before undergoing any treatment.

Book cover design by Beth Anne Campbell.
Edited by Beth Anne Campbell

For all the lost and broken souls. Be kind to yourself.
Peace be with you.

CONTENTS

PROLOGUE

Our history defines who we are, but our choices define who we become.

We all start out in this world like a bicycle wheel. We are born strong and true. We roll along in life and not unexpectedly, we hit a few potholes, speed bumps, and curbs along the way. For many of us, over time, a spoke comes loose, and we start to wobble a little out of true. For a few of us, that spoke is bent or twisted by those who are supposed to be in this world to protect us. It becomes more and more worn with every mile and eventually it breaks, leaving a huge hole in the wheel. One small broken spoke can destroy the balance of the entire bicycle.

I started out like any normal Midwestern kid. I was born in the early 1960s to second-generation immigrant parents. I had two much older siblings and started out my life in rural Michigan surrounded by cornfields, cows, and lakes. My parents owned a small forty-acre farm and a successful dry-cleaning business in the southern part of the state. On paper I probably looked just like any other boy born on a farm at that time.

It all began to unravel when I was sexually abused by my father starting at the age of three and continuing until I was ten years old. The daily physical and verbal abuse from my mother added to the blueprint for my lifelong path of addiction and low self-esteem. Through tenacity, therapy, and forgiveness, I have gone from being a victim—numbing my deep-rooted anger, guilt, and shame with drugs and alcohol—to being a survivor who has been clean and sober since February 25, 2015. Cycling was a big part of that healing process. It gave me an outlet for all the rage I had pent up inside. Racing helped to boost my self-esteem and release the fury within.

I dealt with my own demons in ways that were not healthy. Self-medication is like leaving the bike tire to fix itself. Life will throw you a lot of unforeseen circumstances that can loosen your spokes. By making the decision to commit to healing yourself and allowing others to support you, the scars of your past can be mended, and your wheel can once again become strong and true. Face your demons and the spokes will stay strong.

Although painful to write, I put these words on paper in hopes that my story will help someone get sober or face their demons one day sooner. The need to share my journey with others is a part of my healing process. Perhaps they can find the strength to break free from their addiction and slay their inner demons just as I have. Knowledge, experience, money, time, love, peace...they all answer to the same mantra:

Give it away so you can keep it.

CHAPTER ONE
THE CRASH

There will be good days, bad days, great days, and really shitty ones. Don't allow the actions of others or the events beyond your control put a negative spin on your life. Rise up, smile, move forward. Put it behind you and let it go.

Friday, May 13, 2016

Something hits my right shoulder blade with full force, slamming me onto the bike track where I land on the left side of my face and head. My brain smashes into the right side of my skull. There is a stabbing pain in my left eye just before I lose consciousness. That is my glasses breaking and the frame cutting deeply into my left temple at the corner of my eye. I hit the ground hard.

In my next memory, I am hovering over my own body. The paramedics and my bike racing teammates are circled around me. My wife Marsha is below, standing next to me. Many people are working on my injuries. I don't recall getting loaded into the ambulance and I have only a fleeting memory of riding inside.

I am in the emergency room when I wake up, though I am still not fully aware. My back feels like it is being crushed. As it turns out, spinal boards (those rigid support panels used when spinal or limb injuries are suspected) are not the most comfortable things to lie on. I can see the ceiling, but I am confused about where I am. When I try to look at the floor, I find that I am unable to move my head. Out of the corner of my right eye I can see a little bit of the room and after a few moments I am able to process that I am in a hospital. My head is numb, and I can't figure out how I got here or why.

Marsha is at my side, and she tells me I will be all right. A couple of my teammates come to my side. Nobody wants to talk about what happened. They just tell me I crashed. I keep telling the nurse that my back is killing me and to get me off the backboard. They eventually grant my pleas, to lessen my pain. I keep asking for Coach Paul. He will know what to do.

I don't remember getting released from the ER. I am told I spent the night there. I have fragmented memories of riding home in the car and pulling into our driveway, but I do not remember going into the house. The next three days are a foggy blur. At some point I do talk to Coach Paul on the phone. He tells me to find something alive and focus on it—a plant, a tree, a bird, anything that is living. My co-workers sent me a beautiful plant arrangement with a peace lily and some ivy. It is sitting on my kitchen table where I can see it from the living room. I focus on it. This helps me to start processing thoughts again.

It takes many months to heal my physical injuries. I have over 80 stitches in my face; road rash on both shoulders, elbows, wrists, knees, and on my face; a labral tear in my left shoulder; and a severe concussion. It will take eighteen months to fix my teeth and jaw and three years for the mental fog to clear entirely. It seems like an endless marathon of doctor and dentist appointments. My personal doctor says no surgery, stop racing, avoid brain stimulation, and get plenty of rest.

I do not fully comply.

It is a mere three days before I climb back onto my spin bike. I cannot resist. It is the only place I feel comfortable. Just the motion of moving my legs is enough to give me hope for the future and prevent me from succumbing to the aftermath of my worst crash. And I need hope desperately. I have so many unanswered questions. I have no idea how long it will take to heal or whether I will ever be able to race again. And that scares me. Riding and racing have helped me climb from the depths of Hell. Those two wheels attached to a metal frame have been instrumental in my recovery from the abuse that I suffered at the hands of my parents when I was a child. The thought of never getting on a bike competitively again is beyond comprehension. Riding is almost as much a part of me as my own skin.

One of my teammates later tells me, "I watched you die, and it scared the hell out of me."

Another said he knelt beside me when I was unconscious on the side of the track, took my hand, and kept repeating, "Mike, don't you leave me!"

Yet another says that several riders retired after watching me crash. They can't race anymore. It scared them too much.

After my accident, the race director canceled the rest of the races for the night. That has only happened one other time in the history of the track.

I have seen bad crashes at this level of racing. This one is different. This one is life altering. It is a reminder of my own mortality. And yet, just as it has been with all the other trauma in my past…I will prevail.

It never gets easy; you just get stronger.

SPOKES

Years of racing have taught me to "control what I can control" and it is the mantra I have repeated to myself over the years to remind me that I had no control over what happened to me when I was a child. However, I do have power now over my reaction to that situation.

I don't know if I will ever fully get over the trauma and abuse that I have been through. The best I can do for now is to come to terms with my past. It has shaped who I am as an adult, but it does not have to define me as a person. Our history defines who we are, but our choices define who we become. I choose to become a better version of myself every day.

Life will bring you unforeseen circumstances that alter your course. There will be unexpected results from seemingly insignificant actions. The pain and suffering can be overwhelming. But you must remember that these difficult situations have given you the foundation to become the person you are today, and the person you seek to be. Despite all my tragedies and suffering, I wouldn't trade my past for all the money in the vault. The adversity has made me stronger and given me the tenacity to become who I am today. I am proud of that person.

CHAPTER TWO
BIKES, BEAT-DOWNS, AND BETRAYAL

I went into a deep compartmentalization where my childhood was locked away for decades. And then suddenly it was there.

When I was six years old, I got a brand-new shiny Schwinn Stingray bike in burnt orange with a metallic orange banana seat and matching back rest. I thought it was the coolest bike I had ever seen. I still do, and in fact, I have one nearly identical to it sitting in my home gym today. It reminds me of how far I have come and all the demons I have slain.

I do not remember who gave me that first Stingray. I do remember trying to learn how to ride it. The bike was too big for me at first. Eventually I grew into it but at the start I did not yet have the leg strength to ride up the steep hill of our country driveway. Instead, I would push it up the hill and ride back down. My feet would pedal as fast as I could to take advantage of gravity and get to the highest speed humanly possible before slamming the coaster brake at the very last second to avoid crashing into the chain-link fence that surrounded our yard. Even at that early age I was always testing the limits.

I remember the day I finally learned to ride without training wheels. A close family friend named Lenny was holding me upright and pushing me while I pedaled. Lenny was more of a father figure to me than anyone else in my life at that time. He would jog behind me and offer words of encouragement. Eventually I launched from his guiding hand to a wobbly but solo ride with a grin from ear to ear. That was a sense of freedom I had never experienced before. I knew I had found something that brought me pure joy.

Over time my leg strength improved, and I could finally make it up the steep driveway slope. One of my favorite pastimes was to come racing down the hill and slam on the coaster brake to see how long of a skid mark I could leave on the pavement. With practice, I perfected the art of maximizing my speed and locking the brake just in time to avoid a crash while laying down the most gorgeous patch of black rubber on a sideways slide on the driveway. It was truly a work of art.

It is a miracle that I grew to love bikes at all. The first one I had—a red Western Flyer tricycle that I got for my fourth birthday—was burned in a fit of rage by the woman who gave birth to me. My crime was rolling the tiny front tire over the snow-white sneaker of a visiting cousin while I rode around in the basement. The trike was my very first bike and one of my earliest memories of being at the receiving end of my mother's wrath.

It was 1967 and we were in the basement of our home in rural Michigan. My mother was doing laundry while the cousin—a young man of seventeen or eighteen—kept her company. He was tall and slender and visiting from Chicago where my mother had been born and raised. I was riding my tricycle around the unfinished basement like I always did, racing across the shiny cement floor and circling the support posts as if I were on a bike track.

I was always a bit of a rebel even as a toddler. As I pedaled closer to the cousin, I tried to see how close I could get to his foot. It was a challenge for me, perhaps the first of many competitions with myself that existed only in my mind. *How close can I get my wheel to his shoe?* It became an internal game. My mother told me to stop but I didn't listen. I circled around and made another run at him while she folded sheets. This time I overestimated the distance and ran over his white tennis shoe, leaving the most perfect black tire track over the pristine toe. The imprint was truly striking.

My mother did not see the artistic value. Instead, her anger exploded like a rocket ship into orbit.

"GODDAMN YOU, MIKE! You son-of-a-bitch!"

I had no time to think about escaping before she dropped the sheet mid-fold, yanked me by my ear, and grabbed the tricycle with her other hand. Without so much as a thought to the poor cousin (who must have been horrified), she dragged me out to the burn pit in our back yard—the place where country folk brought their trash to die back then. In one swift movement she doused the bike with lighter fluid, struck a wooden match, and tossed the flame into the pit. I don't even know when or how she got the lighter fluid or matches; it was all one big blur.

As soon as the match hit the pile, my bike became engulfed in flames in one great POOF!

I stood watching in silence as the red and white paint bubbled up and the tires melted into the ground. I wasn't scared or shocked; it was more numbness and despair that I felt. All I could think was, "Wow. My tricycle just burned up." But there were no words, just an overwhelming sense of defeat. At that immature age I could not have understood the underlying rage in my mother or why such a small act set her off like the very blaze she had just ignited.

Spoiler alert: I still don't understand, and I never will. I have accepted that. Now, decades later, I can only continue to try and understand myself.

It was a few years before I would get another bike. But it would not be so long before the next verbal and physical strikes from my mother, or the sexual abuse from my father.

My parents, Mary and Ray, were married in 1940 in Chicago, Illinois. Both were first generation Americans, born of immigrants—my father's family came from Poland while my mother's parents were from Croatia. Both sets of my grandparents arrived in the United States through Ellis Island and the story should have been a classic inspirational immigration tale: Eastern European families make new life in the United States and live the American dream. Somewhere, somehow, something went terribly wrong with that idyllic picture. Mary and Ray's firstborn, my brother Raymond, was born in 1941, and then my sister in 1948. I was the last to arrive, born in 1963, just eighteen months before my brother had his own first child.

Mary and Ray moved to central lower Michigan in the late 1950s, where they raised beef cattle on a large farm with rolling hills and a lake. They also owned and operated a dry-cleaning business with my older brother and sister. The businesses were both thriving, and we never seemed to want for anything, yet my parents were never happy. Our home was a pristine estate from all angles. Beautiful white fence, manicured yard, rolling hills. No one suspected the evil and pain hidden inside those walls.

It would happen in the evening, after dinner.

My mother would tell me to take off my clothes. Using a code word, she would tell me to go see "Papa." While he sat at the dinner table, I would walk over to him timidly, wearing only white briefs, the kind made for innocent little boys. My father would have his pants off, dressed only in his boxers and work shirt. Although it has been many decades, I can still recall the details of the color and print of those boxers. It all seemed so wrong at the time, but I was far too young to understand why. Now that I have had the time and wisdom to process it, I struggle with the most basic questions: *How could a parent do this to their child? How could a parent allow this to happen to their child?* These questions still cannot be reconciled with everything I think of as decent and human.

My father's face was mostly white stubble. It's funny because I refuse to have any facial hair to this day. Sometimes I shave twice in a day just to make sure. The image of him so many years ago is still strong and so wrong in my brain that it impacts the way I look over half a century later. His cheeks hung on his face because he had no teeth. The hair on top of his head was almost gone except for a small rim from ear to ear, which was mostly gray. He was a large-framed man with a big pot belly that would get in the way of the table, so he had to sit back a bit when he lifted me onto his lap. His hands were immense and his fingers thick, almost to the point of being deformed. The ring finger on his right hand had the tip chopped off and there was a small nail that was shaped like a claw sticking out the end. His hands were rough and calloused, both front and back. His forearms were thick but lacking muscle tone. They were once solid and strong, but the effects of age had taken their toll. He always wore a button-down work shirt, usually blue. The white T-shirt underneath was dingy and stained with sweat.

The old man's breath reeked of poor hygiene. In the summer he had a rank body odor that made me want to hold my breath. It wasn't overpowering—more subtle, yet still stifling to a child. He would fondle me for about a half an hour. He always had the newspaper spread across the big round table with the corners hanging off the edge. Likely it was a way for him to hide what he was doing to his helpless, innocent son. I remember looking at the pages of the paper and trying to read and understand the stories. Occasionally there was a photo or sketch to occupy my busy mind. It was a way for me to compartmentalize, to detach from what was going on. I would basically leave my body.

After he got whatever twisted satisfaction he was looking for, he would put me down on the floor like a toy he had gotten tired of playing with. The floor was made of slate and always cold to the touch on my bare feet, even in the heat of summer. I would scamper back to the couch where my mother waited and put my clothes back on. She would hug me and tell me she loved me and kiss me on the cheek or forehead. I would go about playing with my toys as if nothing out of the ordinary had happened. How fucked up is that? How do I even reconcile that? Maybe I never will. I did not know it at the time, but I was learning to compartmentalize. It is a tool I would use for decades to hide from the trauma of the abuse.

I had no feeling either physical or emotional. This was the ritual, night after night. I am certain the detachment is why I can endure tremendous physical and mental pain today. I can separate myself from the moment. I had no clue what I was doing, but now that I am older, I understand it. Detachment was my coping mechanism and I still use it today. When I am in an uncomfortable situation or in physical agony— like when I am racing or training beyond my limits—I find a calm inside of me and detach from the pain of the moment. A warm rush comes over me and my mind becomes clear. I've felt that rush so many times. It's like a warm blanket. Sometimes while in a sprint racing to the finish line I would have the sensation of rising out of my body and observing from above. Detached, calm, and peaceful while the body unleashed a fury of power through the bike.

I remember once asking my mother why the old man always put his hand down my underwear. I'm not sure how old I was, maybe six. Old enough to know that this was not normal. We were both on the couch facing the fireplace. She hugged me and told me it was a tradition from the old country. It was considered an honor for a man to have a son and that fondling was a form of worship, protecting the family by keeping him safe. I didn't understand, and I didn't know what to do. How could I? I wasn't mature enough to mentally process it all. And it didn't matter. It was just another tangled web of lies constantly told to cover up the fact that my father was a pedophile, and my mother was a knowing accessory to the crimes.

My mother had a whole different approach to abuse. It would start out as a slow burn, almost taunting. Then it would escalate to screaming obscenities. Intimidation was her *modus operandi*. Most of the time she would launch into a physical attack after the verbal abuse, armed with whatever weapon was readily available. A corn broom was her favorite. The heavy wooden handle was exactly how she liked it. And the verbal assault didn't stop just because the physical assault had started. I was always a "little bastard" or "little son-of-a-bitch" and it would usually start with "GODDAMN YOU, MIKE!" After countless hours of therapy, meditation, and reflection, I honestly cannot recall ever doing anything that would merit that type of response.

One day, around the age of seven or eight, I was getting ready for school. I was sitting at the kitchen counter breakfast bar when Mary gave me a peanut butter and jelly sandwich for breakfast. To this day I have no idea why I did not want to eat it. It would be years before I realized that I had a nut allergy so bad that one bite could have killed me. I told her I didn't want the sandwich; I wanted a bowl of cereal instead.

After some back and forth she finally relented, shoved the bowl of cereal in front of me, and said with a visceral tone, "There's your fucking cereal! Now eat it and I hope you fucking choke on it!"

I sat there and ate in silence. I was sad because I didn't want to make her mad. I just knew, somehow, that I could not eat the peanut butter.

Not long after this incident, I was heading to the living room from my bedroom, which was on the opposite end of the house. There were only two ways to get there: I could walk straight through the kitchen or go outside and around the house. It never occurred to me to go outside. Why would it? The logical path was through the kitchen. I was on a mission to get to the living room to watch TV. Mom happened to be sweeping the kitchen floor. I paused at the doorway, and she told me to wait. I stopped for a moment until she moved aside to sweep in a corner. I took that as my cue to pass through.

Unfortunately, I misread that signal. She swiftly grabbed me by the right ear and flung me into the corner of the kitchen cabinets where she screamed at me about why I couldn't just listen and do what I was told. As her fury increased, she swapped the ends of the broom and beat me with the handle. Back in those days corn brooms had dense, heavy handles. They were difficult to break, so they made powerful weapons, especially on a defenseless child. I curled up in the fetal position trying to protect my head, which was the focus of her attack. Her onslaught eased for a moment. I peeked out to see her false teeth flying out of her mouth and coming straight at me. If I had not been so terrified, I might have laughed out loud.

Strange as it may seem, I don't remember the physical beatings from Mary hurting very much. I am sure they did, but in comparison to the beatings from my old man they were insignificant. With no teeth, my mother's wrath subsided, and she went on about her day. Not a word was said. I gathered myself up and watched TV quietly, while trying to stay out of the way.

I don't know where my mother's anger came from. I could speculate forever but I will never understand. Maybe it came from her father, my grandfather. There were rumors that he abused her and her younger brother, and that he was an alcoholic. He became incapacitated in his later years, because of the alcohol. He moved in with Ray and Mary in their early marriage years. As I was told, Ray was not happy taking care of his father-in-law. Whether it's true or not, I have no idea. I have been told so many lies that I can't keep track of them. This is why I have so many trust issues. The people I was supposed to rely on the most beat me, molested me, and lied to me. The typical foundation of trust is nowhere near solid.

When my old man got physical, it was brutal. Far worse than a beat down from my mom. For him, it was more ritualistic. As with my mom, I cannot tell you what I ever did to justify his fury. But that fury would rise. He would tell me, "Get your ass downstairs" as he was taking off his belt. The leather was black and narrow with a design etched on it and it made a popping noise as he stripped it from the loops on his pants. To this day I rarely wear a belt, and never a black one. I would scamper down the stairs and wait for the beating.

The basement was a place of secrecy. No one could see the lower level from the main floor. It was dark and unseen. As I have processed it over the years, I believe he took me down there because it was a place where he could hide. He was a big man, and on the outside very tough. Yet he was very secretive about his abuse, like when he spread the newspaper over the table or took me to the basement for punishment. He wasn't tough at all. He was a coward. He wasn't powerful and I'm sure he knew it.

When the punishment was imminent, I never cried or tried to get out of it. There was no use. He would make me pull down my pants and bend over his knee. In just my underwear he would whip my ass with a fury. The belt made a loud crack, and it stung so badly that I screamed in agony. I begged him to stop and promised to be good and never do it again. I still don't know what "it" was.

One time I thought I was going to urinate on his leg as I was getting whipped. I begged him to stop because I had to go. He stopped and pulled down my underwear and told me to stop crying and pee on the floor. I was so distraught I couldn't relax enough to relieve myself. The old man thought I was lying to him, so he whipped me some more.

When the beatings were over Mom would hold me and tell me that he really did love me, and I just had to be good.

I spent as much time outside as possible. It was my refuge. I knew that if I wasn't inside the house, then I wasn't going to get a beat down from one or the other of my parents. They never beat me in public, ever. For them, perception was reality. If all the neighbors thought we had a pristine life with a perfect house surrounded by a white fence and a perfect child, then that's what it was.

What a fucking lie.

Dinner was always a quiet time in my house. We sat around the table with the evening news on the TV, watching Walter Cronkite every single night. My mom never said anything. No one ever asked me what I did at school. No one asked someone else how their day was. There was only silence. When the old man was in the room, you better be at attention with your mouth shut. He was the only one who spoke, and it was always just him complaining about whatever was going on in the world or his life. It was about as far from an idyllic family life as one could possibly get.

After I had eaten everything on my plate (which had been dished up by my mother) I had to get up out of my chair, stand beside the old man and ask for permission to leave the table. We had large wooden chairs with wrap-around arms. They were heavy and difficult to move to and from the table. One evening when I was around thirteen, I was done with dinner, so I stood next to the old man and asked for permission to be excused. He never looked up from his plate, just swung his left hand around with a hook and stabbed me in the right buttock with a fork hard enough puncture my skin.

As he pulled it out, he barked, "I told you to stand up straight. I'm not telling you again!"

You can bet I stood up straight. Tears welled up in my eyes from the excruciating pain. I found out later that he drew blood. I said I was sorry, and the old man told me to go. There was a good sting in my buttock for a while, maybe a week. I realized later that my crime that night was leaning slightly on the arm of his chair. That is what prompted the outburst. My mother never said a word. Ever.

Back then, especially out in the middle of nowhere, we did not have a lot of the services that are available today in the cities and suburbs. My parents kept their abusive behavior locked behind closed doors and the curtains drawn tight. School teachers never noticed what was going on at home. In their defense, they probably weren't trained to look for the signs that seem standard today, like being socially awkward, introverted, emotionally unstable, or bullied. We didn't have Child Protective Services out in the country. I was on an island. I survived by sheer will and learned at an early age how to read people. This served me well in my adult life and gave me the foundation to overcome every obstacle in life presented, even beating addiction by myself.

I only remember someone almost uncovering our dirty little secret once. One night when I was around eight, a neighbor came by unexpectedly. He lived just up the road from us and often chatted with the old man about farming and cattle. On this night his timing was perfect. It was dark, being late fall or winter, and he came to the side door of our house. The curtain happened to be open, so the neighbor stuck his head through, like, "Hey, anyone home?" I was sitting on the old man's lap at the time while he was molesting me. Fear struck immediately. I knew what he was doing to me was wrong, but I didn't know why. I instinctively jumped off his lap, ran over to the couch, and started getting my clothes on because I was just in my underwear. Mary was telling me to hurry up and get dressed before she went to the door. Ray never got up because he wasn't wearing any pants. The neighbor came in, sat down, and my father carried on like nothing was going on. Nothing to see here. The table provided enough coverage that the neighbor was probably none the wiser on what was going on. That was the only time I remember when someone other than my parents might have seen something. If he did, nothing ever came of it.

When I was a kid, I loved to play baseball. I always had a ball and glove in my hand. I would throw the ball against the cement block building of the dry cleaners my parents owned to practice catching fly balls. The building was a tall two-story cinderblock structure just down the hill from our house, and it provided a lot of options for different angles to throw. The business name was prominently displayed high up at one end. The building was painted a pristine white and the letters were a royal blue. It was quite a striking contrast. This was also the best place on the whole building to bounce a baseball.

My nephew Joe and I were messing around one day like normal kids that age do. Joe was only eighteen months younger than me, and we lived just about a mile apart, so we spent a good deal of time together.

We must have been around seven or eight at the time. At some point I threw the ball and hit one of the letters in the sign, breaking the "r" in "Cleaners." My heart plummeted because I knew I was going to be in big trouble. I picked up the broken piece and told my mom what happened. The old man wasn't home, so it would wait until later. She told me it would be all right and to just throw the cracked plastic in the dump.

We had a pile out back of our house where all the non-burnable trash went. It was literally the back of a huge dump truck. The beast barely ran and was a haven for mud wasps until it had to be driven to the back of the farm to empty. Armed with a can of wasp spray, I was responsible for clearing the cab. Fun times (not so much). Those things hurt when they sting and apparently spraying them with wasp killer just pisses them off before they attack, plummet to the earth, and squirm until dead.

I threw the broken "r" into the bed of the truck and the rest of the day passed without incident. The old man later came home, and nothing was said. I thought I had escaped unscathed.

I was wrong.

It was weeks, maybe even a month later. I'm not sure how long; time is inconsequential to a kid at that age. One day the old man noticed the broken "r." He went on a rampage unlike anything I had ever experienced before. It was as if I had burned down the cleaners versus broken a letter on a sign. I was slapped around and dragged to the dump truck, where I was made to rummage through the garbage to find the broken piece, which was only about four inches wide. It was not there. The truck had been dumped at the back of the farm. The broken "r" was gone forever.

After the old man was satisfied that I would not find it, he marched me to the house where a severe beating with the belt followed. I tried to explain that I had just done what Mom told me to do, but there was no redemption simply because I followed orders. It was time for the old man to unleash his fury. He ordered me to pull down my pants and underwear. He never did that before. Whenever I got a beating for something like not putting my toys away, my underwear stayed on. This time was different. His anger had reached a whole new level. As my jeans fell to the floor he yanked me over his knee, pulled down my underwear, and proceeded to beat me with that thin black leather belt that he so loved to vent his anger with. There was no yelling from him, none of the usual rant. Today was different; it was all about vengeance.

Somehow, I had crossed a line with him that I did not know existed. And all the time I wondered, where was my mother? Why didn't she step in? Why didn't she tell him that she had instructed me to put the broken "r" in the truck bed with the other trash. Not only did I get a physical lashing from my father, I also got an invisible "Fuck you!" from my mother. Even at that young age, I knew it was messed up.

SPOKES

Disappointment is a big word. It can have little impact or feel like the weight of the world is on your shoulders. I remember my mother telling me how disappointed she was with me. It would happen when I got in trouble in school or didn't get straight A's on my report card. She often connected it with a very powerful word: shame.

I recall one scolding when I got a grade C. She told me she was very disappointed in me. She said I should be ashamed of this, and that I had to do better. I stood before her, taking the verbal abuse, and hanging my head in disgrace. I could not even look her in the eye. I felt horrible. Mary always pushed me to strive for perfection. I doubt there is such a thing. Maybe in small doses with certain tasks, but not as a whole in the grand scheme of life.

As an adult I carried that burden of disappointment with me. Often, I would catch myself pushing for perfection when it was not an attainable goal. Countless times I placed the burden of disappointment on myself when it should not have even been a thought in my head, or anyone else's head. I was constantly aware of the pressure of letting down those who counted on me to perform at my highest level. To this day I still work on it. Disappointment is a very powerful word. I am learning to let it go, to move past it.

CHAPTER THREE
THE CYCLE OF COPING

To all of those who said I was weak and that I would never make it…I wish you well with your future endeavors.

Amid the constant abuse there were small pockets of normalcy, even joy. When I was ten or eleven, I used to jump off the roof of our house. This may sound odd, but it was one of the few good things I remember about being a boy. Few people ever knew that I did this on a regular basis. I only did it in the summer because in the colder months in lower mid-Michigan the snow would have given me away. Which is ironic because the snow would have also softened the blow.

But maybe that was the point.

I was a wiry kid who could climb like a squirrel. The front of our house had a built-in flower bed adorned with wrought iron ornamental posts strong enough to support my weight. I would climb up using the metal swirls as rungs and flip myself over the gutters onto the roof. I wandered around up there, sitting on the tallest peak and looking out over the farm and countryside. Then I'd walk over the edge on the back side and look over. It was two stories on one side of the house where the walk-out basement door was. It was exhilarating to be at the edge so high.

My parents were usually at the back side of the house where our family room was so I would go up to the front where they couldn't hear me. From there I would walk up the roof five or six feet, get a running start, and launch myself up as high as I could to jump over the edge of the roof. Once I hit the peak of the jump there was a brief moment of non-gravity that gave me the sensation of floating. It was the freest I had ever felt. Then the ground would come rushing up to meet me and with a sharp SMACK I would hit the ground. Because of my light weight, the impact was never enough to break any bones. I learned to roll and lessen the impact, like a stunt man. I spent one summer enjoying those brief moments of weightlessness. It was pure bliss.

I was raised in a Christian household although we didn't practice religion outside the home when I was very young. I don't remember ever attending church until my older brother died when I was six. The old man didn't like it much. Then again, he didn't really like anything. It seemed like he woke up hateful every single day of his miserable life. He was not a religious person, and I never got the sense he was spiritual either.

Mary was the exact opposite. She carried a rosary in her apron pocket, which she almost always wore around the house. She would always tell me she was praying for me. I never really understood why. When I was acting like a normal mischievous child, she would scold me and tell me she could see my "devil horns" sticking out of my hair. As I grew older, I was confused by that. I had always been taught, even in school, that the devil was bad. It was an accepted belief and here I was listening to my mom making references to the devil and me. My confusion only escalated when we started attended a Methodist church as a family when I was a little older. I attended bible study and there I learned how bad the devil was supposed to be. Yet my own mother was constantly calling me "a little devil." I'm still trying to figure that one out. Maybe some things will forever remain a mystery.

Growing up on the farm in rural Michigan gave me many opportunities to explore the outdoors. I also had chores to take care of. One of them was checking the electric fence to ensure it was working properly so the cattle would not get out of the pasture. I had a small current tester that could sense if the fence was working. The chore took me in one big loop around the pasture. In the summer the weeds would grow up to touch the wire and short it out. Then the cattle would push the boundaries for that tiny morsel of grass and eventually knock the fence down. If they got into the road, it could have proven disastrous for both animal and human. Sometimes I would grow tired of using the tester so I would touch the fence. It gave me a small jolt.

One day my childhood friend (who shall remain nameless to

protect the guilty) and I were messing around, being typical goofy ten-year-old boys. We dared each other to touch the wire. It was no big deal for me. I was no stranger to the electrical jolt. We went back and forth for a while. When it was my turn, I had to up the game. I grabbed hold of the wire and held on tight. The electricity ran through my body making it convulse. After what seemed like a minute I let go. I am sure it was not more than five seconds, but it seemed like an eternity as the current ran through me. I must have had a look in my eyes that impressed him. His face was covered with the shock of what he had just witnessed, and he said, "You're crazy!"

From that moment on I had a reputation of being a little *out there*. I still get that today. I accept that. I don't see it as crazy. I see it as driven. I am willing to take it to the next level without concern for the level of pain. All that matters is the result. Doing what others won't so I can achieve what others can't.

Another of my regular chores was to fill the water trough and check the cattle at the West Farm. It was an eighty-acre parcel separate from our main farm about a mile up the road. There were several sizeable hills between the two farms that made it seem like it was uphill in both directions. I remember speeding down the first hill on my bike to get a good run up the next hill and repeat until I got there. It was a blast! Every evening, I would repeat this ritual of checking the cattle and making sure the water trough was full. I spent a lot more time out there than was required to complete the chores. It became my escape. Nobody messed with me there. It was my own time and space and one of the few times I felt free and safe.

The sexual abuse from my father stopped when I was ten or eleven but the physical abuse from both parents continued a bit longer. I took my last beatdown from Mary when I was twelve. Thirteen seemed to be the tipping point when Ray no longer viewed me as a child but as finally entering the phase of manhood. I had a sizeable list of chores that I was responsible for on the farm. In addition, I had a steady job working in the dry cleaners six days a week doing various janitorial tasks. The store front was open at six a.m. on weekdays. One of my duties was to greet the customers and receive/disperse clothes for a couple hours each morning before school. Not only did this instill a strong work ethic but I learned how to interact with people. It taught me how to read body language and the message they were sending without using their words. For my efforts I received a small allowance. Responsibility and money gave me a small sense of freedom and self-worth.

As my teenage years progressed, I went to town daily to pick up and deliver dry cleaning to our drop stations. The morning run was a quick in-and-out of town. Later there would be more pickups and deliveries and then counting the register and bringing back the daily revenue. This gave me my first real business experience—interacting with adults, earning their respect, and learning who to trust. Or at least, who to believe. I also learned how to count money and balance the register every day.

During the evening runs, I had many opportunities to experience city life. As I grew older, I started to identify the dealers, pimps, and gangs. I remember their cars—Lincolns and Cadillacs mostly—and they were immaculate. It was during this time that Lenny—who worked for our dry-cleaning business and was a Vietnam veteran—taught me street smarts. I learned how to recognize potential danger, how to avoid it, and how to be more aware of the world around me. These were not formal lessons taught in a class. It was more creating an awareness of my surroundings and continuously assessing the environment. These were skills I had learned earlier in life in a futile attempt to avoid the abuse at home. Lenny taught me subtle things, like how a person walks down the sidewalk means something. A quick step means they are moving through or away from something or someone. A slower walk but glancing over their shoulder could mean they are expecting trouble and want to be ready. One hand in their coat pocket could mean they have a weapon. All this could mean something or maybe it all adds up to nothing. Either way, if you are aware then you can avoid the situation or strike first to gain control.

When I was fourteen, I was really into hunting. It was my escape from the hell of my home. Because we lived on a lake, I had easy access to waterfowl. I got it in my head that if I got a black Labrador retriever, I could train him to hunt with me. Whenever I shot waterfowl, they would fall into the lake. I would then have to paddle the boat out to pick them up. I thought if I had my own dog, I could train it to retrieve the birds. This would be a cool project! Lenny had a Golden Retriever and I had helped him train it a few years earlier, so I figured I was up to it. We already had two robust kennels left over from the Dalmatians and St. Bernard's we had raised when I was growing up. My older brother had been the dog person in the family. The old man hated them. All the more reason for me to succeed with raising and training my own. It was my way of saying, "Fuck you." After a lot of persistence, he finally gave in. There was a list of rules about the upkeep of the kennel, care for the dog, etc. I didn't need to be told. I was motivated.

For some reason, I wanted an AKC registered black Labrador retriever. It had to be black, I have no idea why. Or maybe I do. My father was racist at a depth I had never seen in my life. He hated black people with a passion. He would even curse his black cattle just because they were black. So maybe instinctively, getting a black dog was another "Fuck you."

I found a kennel not too far from home. They charged $125.00 for a registered male. Back in the 1970s that was a lot of money. Of course, there was no way the old man was going to contribute a dime, so I saved my allowance. By the time I had enough money, I was fifteen years old. My parents took me to the kennel. There was a new litter. I picked out what I felt was the best one…or maybe he picked me out. I named him Ace Frehley after the KISS rock band guitarist. I was really into KISS at that era of my life.

Ace and I were inseparable. I trained him to retrieve, and we were hunting the next season. It was awesome! When Ace was only about a year old, he got sick suddenly and died the next day. I doubt we had given him shots or vaccines as we should have, that was just the way of country folk back then. I vaguely remember someone saying "heartworm," but it might have been Lenny giving me something for closure. I didn't even have time to figure out if I should call the vet before Ace died.

Around this time in my mid-teens, I often rode my motorcycle through the pasture. I wasn't allowed to take it on the road until after I was sixteen, so I would ride down the big grassy hills as fast as the motorcycle would go and get as close to obstacles as I possibly could. It was like a game for me to see how close I could get to crashing without actually doing so. I had no regard for injury and would launch off jumps that would leave me suspended ten feet or more in the air. The suspension on bikes back then was not like it is today. They took a beating, and so did my body. After I got my motorcycle license, I would ride the back roads. They were all gravel, and I could fly. I had little fear of high speeds or the consequences of a potential crash.

One day I was riding through a hay field on a well-known trail I had built. I came flying down a little hill which launched me into a much larger hill, which allowed me to get some serious air off the top. I didn't know it, but a groundhog had burrowed a home in the middle of my trail. I never saw it coming. My front wheel hit the hole and stopped hard, immediately launching me over the handlebars like a yard dart at fifty miles per hour. I face-planted in the dirt and everything went black. I have no idea how long I was knocked unconscious. I woke up with extreme pain throughout my chest. I couldn't breathe. I lay there, assessing the damage.

Finally, I pulled myself together and the breathing returned, along with reality. I could not move my left arm. I limped back to the bike and tried to pick it up using only one arm. I was scrawny back then, as I was already well into excessive alcohol and drug use. The bike was a Kawasaki 175 Enduro. It was not built for light weight. I struggled to pick the bike up and ride back home. This was well before the age of cell phones, and I doubt anyone even knew where I was. They wouldn't even know where to begin looking for me. I was way back in the fields, hidden from the nearest road. It wasn't like someone would eventually drive by and see me lying there. I had to find my own way out. The handlebars were bent almost to the point where I could not ride. But I decided it was doable, and my only option.

I struggled to get the bike started and had to push through the excruciating pain in my left shoulder. The clutch was on the left, which made it even harder. I had to reach across with my right arm and engage the clutch, then barely hold it with my injured arm. After I got rolling, I could use my foot. Somehow, I managed to get home. I could hardly walk up the stairs to get cleaned up. Just taking off my clothes to shower invoked screams of agony. I suspect it was a bruised collarbone. I've had countless x-rays since then and nothing has shown as a fracture or break. But sometimes bruised bones hurt more than broken ones. When I hit ground out in the field, I tumbled like a rag doll, so it hurt everywhere.

I was grateful that my mother was not there when I got home. I got myself cleaned up as best I could and tried to pull myself together. I still had to go to town to our drop stations to pick up cleaning for work. It was my job to make the evening run on Saturdays, which meant delivering and picking up clothes and closing out the till. At one of the drop stations I ran into Lenny.

"Mike, what the fuck did you do? What did you take?"

He was certain I had taken mind-altering drugs, that's how bad I looked. I explained to Lenny what had happened and how bad I crashed. He did a physical assessment of my upper body and seemed satisfied that nothing was broken. Breathing was still a challenge, and I couldn't fully inflate my lungs, but I powered through to get the job done. I assume my mother found out eventually, but I don't recall much about it. Not that she would have done anything.

I never went to the hospital. I just took another hit of speed, drank more whiskey, and tried to move forward. That is what addicts do. We self-medicate, ignore the pain, and fool ourselves into believing it will go away. But it is always there, dangling off the rear bumper, popping up when you least expect it and are least prepared for it. The only way to get past that pain is to face it head on and deal with it. Easier said than done, I know. *It never gets easy; you just get stronger.*

There have been numerous other self-destructive behaviors over the years, all tied back to my childhood. I would not realize it for decades, but all these things were a mask for all the abuse I was subjected to from my earliest memory. I took my first drink at age fourteen. At fifteen I smoked my first cigarette and my first joint. I graduated to pills at sixteen, and at seventeen I dropped acid for the first time. By the time I was legally able to vote I was hooked on speed. I didn't know it at the time, but I was trying to numb the pain. I had nobody to turn to and the booze and drugs offered me a little relief from the shame and guilt. I know now that I had nothing to be ashamed of. But back then, I had not faced the demons and felt like it was all my fault.

SPOKES

There is something inside my DNA that fuels indulgence in excess. As a child I would chug cola until it ran out my nose. It was a competition game that my friends and I would play. Who could guzzle a bottle the fastest? I always took every competition to the extreme. Playing cowboys and Indians involved BB guns and real arrows. It's a wonder we didn't kill each other. And somehow, I got away with it.

In my later years I developed a mantra: Do what others won't so I can achieve what others can't. Maybe that mantra began when I was a child and developed over a lifetime of hard work. Even as a kid I really had no fear of getting injured, nor did I recoil from the possibility of getting hurt. I guess when you grow up in a house filled with pain you become calloused to the pain life can give you. Maybe the mental abuse overrides the physical abuse, and the mental pain makes the physical pain seem insignificant.

Maybe…

CHAPTER FOUR
THE RECKLESS YEARS

The hate is what I am still learning to let go of, and it's fucking hard. I know if I don't, it will eat me from the inside.

My father died in 1981, just three days after my dog passed away. I cried when Ace died. I mourned his death. I did not do the same for the old man.

Just prior to this, I had been on the edge of the dark pit of addiction. I could sense that the old man was old and frail. He was dying and I didn't care. I was smoking a pack of Camel Filters a day; smoking pot daily; popping speed several times a week; and drinking on the weekends. After he passed, the only disciplinarian in my life was Mary and she lost her grip on me while dealing with the loss of her husband.

I was sixteen when he took his last breath, and I spiraled out of control. The drugs, drinking and excess indulgence went off the charts. At the same time, I lost the presence of the only strong male role model in my life, our family friend Lenny. Lenny had succumbed to his own addiction. He was dealing with his own demons and had made many bad choices. As a result of his substance abuse, he lost his marriage, his job, his family, and who knows how much more. He eventually moved away.

Lenny was a strong man physically who loved the outdoors. He was more of a father figure in my life than my old man. Don't get me wrong...Lenny was no saint. I lifted my first cigarette and chew from him: Red Man and Camel non-filtered. Camel Filters would be another addiction for the next fifteen years of my life. I smoked pot with Lenny on a regular basis. I drank cheap wine with him while we watched *Saturday Night Live*. Lenny introduced me to speed, which would grow to be one of the most damaging vices I ever had. I was beyond fucked up, always looking for the next high or trying to maintain the one I was in. I put no blame on Lenny. It wasn't him who got me addicted; it was me. If he had not been there and played that role, someone else would have.

As I slipped deeper into the death grip of addiction, I was the instigator of my indulgence. Lenny would warn me to back off or stop the excessiveness. I never listened. I had my own dealers. I was hiding from my own pain. Lenny gave me a safe environment in which to party. We would hang at his house and watch TV or go out to an old pickup truck in the field and get high, drink wine, and talk about life. It was almost like he was protecting me from the streets.

I saw Lenny only twice before he passed away years later from complications due to his compulsions. He wasn't perfect and did things that ultimately resulted in him not being a part of our family anymore. But he was still a better father figure than the pedophile whose DNA I happen to share.

Let's talk about the death of my old man. I honestly didn't care. And I still don't, other than the fact that I never got the chance to confront him for what he did. He was an evil person who had no place on this earth. He ruined lives. He bullied people. He sexually molested an innocent child. I have no idea where this all came from. His way of dealing with life was to dominate and control every aspect of it. Every day was filled with bitterness.

When I got the phone call from the hospital about the old man, I handed the receiver to my sister. I didn't need to be told the news. I already knew. I didn't even cry. In truth, it was a relief when he passed. I wouldn't have known how to deal with his death even if I had cared. My mother was a train wreck. I had no foundation for any type of grief, so instead I compartmentalized it. I was finally out from under his iron fist.

The old man died the summer before my senior year of high school. I was living at home at the time. Mary was on me to get clean. I don't think she was fully aware of everything I was taking or how bad it really was, but she knew I was an addict. The only thing I wanted was to be free from the constraints of all authority figures and to get a job. I would have quit school but knew I would have to move out of my house. This was a dealbreaker. As bad as it was living with my mother, I wasn't willing to be homeless. At sixteen with no job, that wasn't a great option.

Shortly after Ray died, we liquidated the dry-cleaning business. A few months before, knowing the end was near and inevitable, he had auctioned off all his cattle and farm equipment. The farm was gone, the business was gone. I really didn't have anything to motivate me. In addition to dealing with the loss of a father who wasn't a father and losing

Lenny from my life, I was also trying to navigate the collapse of my daily structure. We no longer had the dry cleaners. There were no farm chores. I no longer had to get up early in the morning even during the school year and work both of our businesses. All of that was gone. My daily rhythm had vanished.

Being so busy for so many years had helped to deflect the thoughts and memories of the abuse. Now I was decidedly un-busy and that left a lot of brain space. I was not ready enough or mature enough to deal with that trauma. So, I devolved deeper into a life of drugs and alcohol and self-destructive behaviors. Every day I was smoking pot and every weekend I was blind drunk. I skipped so much school that I had Saturday detention every week of my senior year. For me it was a good tradeoff. Regular school was all day and there was accountability. Saturday detention I could show up hungover or high or both and nobody cared. It was a half-day and we got smoke breaks. I figured, if I have to do the time then it might as well be easy time.

Eventually my sister stepped in to help Mary keep me from total self-destruction. She would ask me about what I was doing and where I was going. She bluntly asked me how much pot or drink or speed I did. At one point I even went to a psychiatrist. I sat in the office while the doctor asked me questions about my addiction. I lied my way through it with utter sincerity. None of this helped and only made me more aware. My sister was more street smart than Mary, which made the deception more challenging. In the end it is likely that everyone knew but lacked the ability to deal with my addiction. I graduated 98th out of 102 in my class with a GPA around 2.0. I honestly think they just didn't want me back, so they gave me a diploma. It's not that I was dumb; I just didn't care.

I eventually got a part time job in a grocery store. After a few months, I had screwed that up by missing work and coming to work high. By the grace of God, I got a call from a former teacher telling me about another job lead. I applied and got the position. It was a factory job, assembly line work in an auto parts manufacturing plant. Mindless work, but it paid well. While it was a good move financially, it also allowed me unrestricted access to drugs and alcohol. By then I was just seventeen and my coworkers were all over twenty-one. Equipped with party experience and a fake ID there was no slowing the train of self-destruction. My coworkers took partying to a whole new level. I quickly became one of the crew and the wicked mistress of addiction put her death grip on me. The drugs were better and more plentiful than I had experienced before. The booze was never-ending. Before I knew it, I was popping speed to stay awake and popping sleeping pills to get to sleep. A pill to get up. A pill to go to down. Or rather, a handful of pills. It was a constant roller coaster of highs and lows. My stomach was so torn up from the pills and booze that I started snorting the speed instead of swallowing it to keep me going. My mood was erratic and aggressive. I didn't know who I was anymore.

In 1983, for my twentieth birthday, I threw a huge party to celebrate the end of my teens. I knew a guy who had a local band, so we got them booked and someone got twenty kegs of beer. There were fliers posted all over town. There must have been over three hundred people at the venue, which was the empty building adjacent to my house that once was our livelihood. The cleaning business had closed down when my father died a couple years earlier, and it was now just cement-block walls and an empty floor. The nephew of the guy who was currently renting the building organized the band and someone's dad financed the booze. There was a three-dollar cover charge for all you could drink. There were so many vehicles that the road was down to one lane. Cars were parked in the pasture behind the cleaners and my house. The building was wall-to-wall people…so many that I could barely carry my beer through the crowd.

The party went on into the wee hours. There were fights and drunken debauchery. It was like a mini-Woodstock. I remember walking over to my house around midnight and saw several men and women urinating on Mary's front lawn. For just a moment there was a little karma in the world. Someone spraypainted graffiti on the driveway of the cleaners. Later, the cops showed up and shut it down. I'm sure it was one of the neighbors who called them. The partygoers dispersed, and the birthday bash was over.

The trash left behind filled multiple pickup trucks. It was surreal. It took about a week to clean up and I think I only had one friend who helped me. It had rained that night, so the pasture was all torn up from the cars driving through the mud. The wrath of my mother was off the charts. She screamed at me for days, complaining about the garbage and telling me to get sober. After a few days it was the silent treatment. At no time during this period in my life did I think that I was an addict. I was in too deep. I had zero thoughts about cutting back or quitting. It never entered my mind. My only thought was "More."

A few weeks later, in late November of 1983, I met the woman who would become my wife and my life took a turn for the better.

SPOKES

With a broken past, there have been countless times when I wished I could erase my history and write a clean story. However, as I processed my healing and faced my demons, I realized that my brutal past has made me the strong person I am today. Without the pain there would be no drive. Without the pain there would be no pursuit of life with a passion. Without the pain there would be no "ME!" Don't get me wrong; I would not wish my past on anyone. No one should have to endure what I have been through.

Once I learned to let go of the hatred, the pain eased, and the healing began. I still struggle with that from time to time. The letting go part. Fortunately, therapy, meditation, and faith have all contributed to my recovery. I know that if I don't let go of the hate, it will destroy me from the inside out. Once I accepted that and embraced that concept, a sense of peace crept into my life in every aspect. I never lost the drive or the passion. Quite the opposite; the passion for life flourished. And I now have gratitude for all that I have been through and each day that I am given.

CHAPTER FIVE
MANAGING IT ALL WITH MARSHA

Honesty with everyone is very important. I believe there are three people in your life you should be candidly and painfully honest with on every topic. In no particular order: your spouse, your doctor, the person in the mirror.

Through all the bad choices I've made in my life, I have had an angel of mercy to see me through all my sins. Her name is Marsha.

When I first met Marsha, it was a cold, late-autumn day in Michigan. Her maroon Oldsmobile had a flat tire in front of the house I still shared with my mother. Marsha had no idea how to change it and she didn't have anyone to call for help. I took care of the tire because I liked her smile and the way her jeans fit. Even now, a lifetime later, I still do. Marsha wanted to pay me for helping her, but I already had enough party money to keep me satisfied. She had one of her young sons with her, and I could tell she wasn't well off. At some point in our conversation, she mentioned being recently divorced. I politely declined the money but told her she could have my phone number and take me to dinner sometime. Imagine my surprise when she accepted. I might have just met my match.

Our first date was a week later. Dinner, movie, and drinks ended with sex and cigarettes. There is something special about unattached sex when you are young. I rarely dated anyone my age after high school. I didn't have time for the drama. All I wanted was a good buzz, sex, and cigarettes. Older women—mostly divorced single mothers—wanted the same thing. HIV/AIDS wasn't an issue yet, so sexual freedom wasn't an item of concern. Life was good. That's why Marsha and I hit it off so well in those early days. We wanted the same things: a good time, to party, and no drama. It just worked.

One date with Marsha led to another and after only a few months, we officially moved in together. I had quasi moved in with her in February, at her parents' home (they were in Florida). The parents were returning in spring, so we had to figure something out by then. My sister was renting out a house close my childhood home, so we worked out a deal and Marsha and I moved in there before her parents came back. They were none the wiser.

Marsha and I were both carefree spirits and we enjoyed each other. She grew to be my soulmate and the foundation of my stability. She had an easy way about her that took the edge off my addiction. She *soothed* it. Marsha never judged; she was my angel of mercy. I didn't get sober or clean, I just slowed down. I was still drinking a lot, but I had mostly laid off the speed and was smoking a lot less pot. The drinking was also focused more on the weekends and even then, it wasn't constant blackout drinking.

Marsha had a way about her that was comforting. Just having her near me calmed me and kept me from going over the edge. I felt less rage inside with her by my side. As the years rolled by, I became a stronger role model for the boys. Marsha had two sons by her previous marriage. They were three and six years old when I entered their lives. I was not prepared to be a father figure. I had lost all the men in my life who might have shown me the way. The one who should have been my guide was instead a monster. But somehow, I figured it out on the fly, without that history to draw from. In the end it all worked out. Funny thing about life; it always works out as it should.

Eventually I got the urge to have a child of my own, but we both wanted to get married before bringing another life into the world. So, in the same spontaneous fashion that we had lived our lives, we decided to marry on my birthday. It was a bitter cold November day much like the first day we met. We went to the courthouse and said our vows in front of two county clerks, who were our only witnesses. It was low key but satisfying. Afterwards, Marsha and I went to my mother's house to tell her the news. We were standing at the door and despite our past, I was excited to tell her the happy news. All she said was, "I'm not watching those kids." No congratulations. No welcoming Marsha officially to the family. Just bitterness.

Marsha and I took a long weekend and never left the hotel room.

My relationship with Mary during that time was a roller coaster. She was no longer able to abuse me as I was now a grown man of twenty-two and starting my own family. But she still tried to manipulate and control. Those were the tools she had, so she would use them. On Saturday nights she might be angry at me because I had a bonfire with some friends. Then she'd come over on Sunday morning to have coffee. She did have a superficial relationship with the kids, being the sweet grandmother who gave them candy and such. But if we ever needed a babysitter to go out for a night, she would refuse. She used the control and manipulation to continue the abuse that had started before I even had memories.

People might wonder how I could sit at the table with this person who had enacted such verbal, physical, and psychological abuse for so many years. The truth is, I had compartmentalized a lot of it. I had buried my past so deeply that it wasn't even a fleeting thought. I didn't think about it. I learned much later, through therapy, that this kind of behavior is textbook. It would be nearly three decades before I finally faced my past and started to heal.

My mother's words still ring in my head "I fucking hate you! I disown you! Don't ever come around me again!"

This wasn't the first time I'd heard them, and they usually came after a bout of excessive drinking. No excuses.

I was twenty-three years old. It was the night before Christmas Eve and I had a few days off work, so my alcohol consumption was at peak intake. Marsha and I were still renting the house down the road from my childhood home, where my mother still lived. Though the cattle were gone, Mary still owned the land and there was plenty of room in the pasture and on the large lake for riding snowmobiles and All-Terrain Vehicles (ATVs).

One of my drinking buddies—let's call him Buddy—was visiting. We'd had quite a few and it was around midnight. I thought it would be a good idea to take his snowmobile and my three-wheeled ATV for a ride on the lake. Buddy didn't have a muffler on his sled. It was LOUD! Mary's house was about a half mile away from the lake. Buddy and I had been racing around the farm and lake for about an hour when my mother drove her car through the snow-covered pasture and chased us down. She jumped out of the car when we stopped and started a screaming rant. The names she called me were venomous. And with her parting comment, she disowned me. Yes, once again I had been disowned (no, this wasn't the first time). It's a running joke in the family that I have the record for being disowned the most times. I wear that badge with pride.

We were scheduled to celebrate Christmas Eve at her house later that day. My step-kids were looking forward to it. Now I had screwed it up with my drunken actions. After I slept it off, I told Marsha what happened, and she laughed. She said I was the only one that could get disowned on Christmas Eve. Yeah, I'm the only one with a mom who is off-the-charts crazy. I called Mary and apologized before the event so the kids could have a good Christmas.

I realize that my actions were irresponsible. Perhaps even reckless. However, even now as a parent I cannot reconcile her reaction to my behavior. Beat downs heal but words never leave the echo of your mind. A lifetime later and those words still ring in my head like they were spoken an hour ago. *It never gets easy; you just get stronger.* Learning forgiveness has been a hard lesson, one that I am still working on. Letting go of the hate is the hardest thing I've ever had to do but I know it will eat me alive from the inside out if I don't.

Harsh words like getting disowned from my mom not only changed my relationship with her; they changed me. Hearing the verbal abuse as a child gave me a different perception of right and wrong and how to treat people. It impacted relationships in later years. As I grew older, I realized that treating people with respect was the path to successful relationships. It is interesting how as a child, adolescent, and young adult I was treated with utter disrespect by those closest to me— my own parents, who were supposed to love me and teach me how to treat others. Yet ironically, their verbal and physical abuse taught me compassion and respect. As an adult I treat everyone with respect until they show me that they do not deserve it. Then I simply stop associating with them. Those are not my people. I just walk away. When I am in a public place, and I see someone treating another with disrespect, I bristle. It takes all my self-control to not step in and make right what I see as wrong. As with many things in my life, the negative has been turned into a positive. Today I am a better man for all the pain I have endured.

Despite being "disowned" by my mother, I stuck around for a few years. I still had not acknowledged the abuse I suffered from her and from my father. The coping mechanisms were very well in place and alcohol was front and center of it all. As much as I might try to deny it, drinking was becoming increasingly problematic.

One cold fall night in Michigan changed the course of my life. I was out with two of my best drinking buddies from Detroit. We were cruising the back roads in their pickup truck drinking tall boy Miller, a.k.a. *tall blondes*. Yes, we even had nicknames for our booze. A pint of peppermint schnapps was getting passed around as well. Somehow, we ended up at the town sports bar where we met up with all the local alcoholics for even more overconsumption. It was past midnight by the time we left. I was blind drunk and still had to make it to work at six a.m. I crawled into the back seat of the crew cab pickup and passed out.

When I woke up, my friend Slim told me they were lost. I tried to figure out where we were and didn't recognize any landmarks. I said, "Fuck you guys!" and crawled through the small slider window in the back to the bed of the truck. The cool air felt good…a quick rush of adrenaline that seemed to sober me up a little. It was deceptive. Nothing but time would truly bring me closer to coherence. I went to the tailgate and bent over it, holding on with both hands. I thought I could jump out when the truck slowed down and then walk home. The pavement was rushing under the truck. Slim took a corner rather fast and jerked the wheel. The truck shifted under me, and I lost my balance. Everything moved in slow motion as the road got closer. I was heading for a face plant on the pavement at thirty-five miles per hour! In that instant I DID immediately sober up, at least enough to comprehend my inevitable pain. My hands were desperately trying to grip the tailgate to keep me from falling. But my fingers failed. The left side of my face landed on the asphalt with a loud SMACK!

Everything went black and numb in an instant. I rolled into the ditch. I lost my glasses and couldn't see. All I could think was, "I've got to get home and get cleaned up for work." I crawled up out of the ditch and stumbled to the road, where I started walking. Or really, stumbling. I didn't know where I was. Later I realized that I had fallen off the truck just over a mile from home, on a curved road adjacent to the one I lived on. At the time, though, I was lost. The pain was excruciating. I was bleeding profusely from my face. I knew I was in a bad place, but panic never set in. Most of my teeth on the left side of my mouth were gone and I was spitting out blood and tooth fragments. Still, I kept walking. By the grace of God, I was heading in the right direction. A lone car passed. I tried to flag them down, but they just kept going. I don't blame them. I must have looked like something from a horror movie.

Slim eventually came back to look for me. I climbed into the cab, and he took me home. I stood in front of the bathroom mirror, head swollen, left eye swelled shut, a bloody mess, and barely able to talk. While I was trying to get cleaned up, Marsha came rushing in with panic all over her face. She said I had to go to the hospital, but I resisted. Even after seeing the damage, I was convinced I was invincible and just needed some rest. Eventually, though, I agreed. I had a few seconds of clarity during which I realized I wasn't going to be able to sleep this off like I had done a million other blackout drunk nights. I needed professional medical care. So, we all piled into Slim's truck. Slim had stayed around until Marsha figured out what to do. He was sober by now and Marsha was in no condition to drive. I was on the verge of passing out several times on the twenty-mile ride to the nearest hospital. Marsha kept telling me to stay awake. I was so out of it that I didn't even think to ask who was watching the kids.

When we got to the emergency room, my blood alcohol content tested at 0.8 percent, which is ten times the legally intoxicated limit by today's standards. The doctors said I should have been dead, if not from the crash, then from alcohol poisoning. They couldn't give me any pain killers until I sobered up. The cops even showed up. They questioned me hard, thinking I had been beat up. Nope, just drunk and stupid. The ER had called them because they thought there was more to the story than me being an intoxicated idiot.

I spent the next two days recovering in the hospital thinking about getting sober. I knew that I had to do something if I was going to keep all that was dear to me. I had a son now. I had a family to support. I had a good job and a wife who loved me and cared about me. I had everything to lose and nothing to gain by continuing down this path.

The hospital nurses made me promise to go to get help. Rehab wasn't popular at that time. It wasn't a topic anyone talked about, and I certainly didn't know anyone who had gone to rehab. I promised them I would, but I knew it was a lie even as the words rolled off my tongue. I wanted a mirror, but nobody would give me one. Eventually I got a vague look at myself through the back of a balloon with a silver surface. I did look like something out of a horror movie. My head was twice as big as it should be, and my left eye was swollen shut. I had stitches in my upper lip and my entire face was puffy and bloated. That lone car was right to take a hard pass when I was stumbling down the road. Given the situation and the severity of my injuries, I should not be alive.

A good friend and mentor of mine stopped by. He was a decorated Marine in the Vietnam War. I knew he had seen the worst that humanity had to offer. He was a hard man who had taught me how to shoot better. There was no gray area with him, only black and white. He later told me I looked worse than anything he had seen in combat.

When I got home, I hit rock bottom. Until then I hadn't accepted that sobriety was necessary for future survival. I was lying on the couch recovering when my two-year-old son saw the real me for the first time. I wanted to hug him, but he was terrified. He started to whimper and back away. Marsha comforted him and told him it would be all right.

That is the moment when I hit my lowest point. That's when I knew I had to get sober. I wouldn't touch another drop of alcohol for the next fifteen years.

SPOKES

Marsha is a Saint. If she were not in my life I would either be dead or living on the streets. She is the only woman who ever loved me unconditionally. I cannot begin to find words to adequately describe all that she has given me: absolute love, forgiveness, a million second chances, a soft place to land, and a hug. Unconditional love is rare. It is even more uncommon in the life of an addict. Somehow Marsha always finds it in her heart to forgive. There is no greater gift one can receive from another person.

We have all heard the saying "Behind every good man is a good woman." I respectfully disagree. My life with Marsha is a partnership, a team effort. For all the times I have been strong, Marsha has been beside me. Never "behind" me. Whenever I am weak, Marsha is there, encouraging me to rise up and move forward. She doesn't coddle me when I cross a line or fail miserably. On the contrary, she is the first in line to light me up and tell me how stupid I have been. But after the fireworks displays that only a redheaded woman can deliver, she always shows empathy and encouragement to do the right things moving forward. She always chooses forgiveness over bitterness.

Marsha loved me even when I didn't love myself. She believed I was capable of more than I had accomplished. Marsha saw the strength in me that I didn't believe I had. She supported my self-esteem. It has been a lifelong struggle to trust that she was right. I am stronger than I think I am. I can achieve more than I give myself credit for. Marsha believes in me...always. She is without a doubt the most tolerant, understanding, forgiving, and loving person I have ever known. I would not be alive today without her.

CHAPTER SIX
THE LONG ROAD TO SEATTLE

Risk it all every day. There may not be a tomorrow. When the end comes you will regret the things you did NOT do far more than the things you DID do.

I left Michigan and my broken past behind in 1991. There was nothing there that I ever needed to see again. It's not that I don't have good memories. I do have some. I have family there whom I love very much. I have great memories of hanging out with friends, learning to hunt, having a few great mentors. But there is always a shadow hanging over all of that. I feel cheated that my parents put me in a position where I had to choose leaving the people I loved to avoid the pain. But it had to be done. So, I left.

It was two years after the truck accident when we moved on. I had spent a year of that time recovering from the accident and getting some extensive reconstructive dental work. I was still working at the tool company with the same guys I had partied with before, but I was not drinking myself. That makes for a horrible recovery. Things were not great at work otherwise. It was a shit train ready to go off the rails. I had been there for ten years and was getting restless. I had been doing a little farming at the time, but it was too expensive to launch my own business. There was nothing left for me there, so we made the decision to leave.

The things in my life that were of greatest value went with me: Marsha and our children. It would be many years before I returned to my home state, and that was only out of respect for Marsha's parents. I had nothing to say to anyone in my family. I had moved on. Or so I thought. It would be another decade before I realized just how broken I was. It would be two more decades before I realized how strong I had been to walk away.

For a long time, I always thought I had run away from the pain. In truth, it had just followed me. I now realize that the memories from my past that I thought I had put in the rear-view mirror were stuck to the bumper, dragging along behind me, and occasionally popping up to remind me of how broken I really was. It took a lot of courage and strength to leave in 1991. I had spent my entire life living within a half mile of where I grew up. I had never traveled more than a couple hundred miles from home and even those short trips were rare. I could not have found the inner strength to move without my wife.

At this stage in my journey, I was still compartmentalizing the abuse from my childhood. Maybe *suppressing* is a better word. In any case, I was not fully conscious or aware of my past. I never gave it a thought. I had not yet acknowledged how broken I was. As a result, I found myself restless and unable to find true happiness. I had given up the alcohol and drugs but that left gaps that had to be filled to keep those bad thoughts dormant. I had not yet reconnected with the bike or developed an exercise regimen to help ease the pain of my past.

When we decided to leave Michigan, I was working at the dead-end factory job and still in the shadow of my mother, literally and figuratively. With Marsha and I living painfully close to my childhood home, it was hard to be free. It was impossible for me to be an independent adult or to become my own person. I was constantly watched, my every move scrutinized. I was too close to my past.

And that proximity wasn't just measured by physical distance. I also had a passion for livestock farming. I enjoyed the freedom of the outdoors, and the hard work was rewarding. Growing up on a beef cattle farm had laid the foundation. But cattle were too close to what my father had done. I had to look for something different enough to separate me from my abuser. Over the years I had raised a few pigs, and I liked the experience. So, after ten years in the factory I walked away from a steady paycheck and took a job on a large pig farm an hour away in Ohio. We made plans to move, and our adventure began.

I worked in Ohio for three years while my hunger continued to grow. I had learned a great deal and now wanted more responsibility—which I thought would equate to more money and success. Little did I know that all of this was possible but only at the price of more headaches. In 1994 I took another job on a larger pig farm in Missouri. Each new adventure was fun for the entire family in different ways. The kids found new friends. Marsha and I explored new countryside. Marsha had a horse from our Michigan farm, and we were always around cows, pigs, chickens, and goats. It was a safe environment in which to raise a family.

Then the newness of the Missouri adventure eventually wore off and I was restless again. About every three years I would get the urge to move on to something new. I don't know why three years was the magic number, but that was the cycle. I would start a new position with motivation and excitement. At around two and a half years in, I would start getting the urge again and we would make a change. I didn't know that I was running away from something or maybe searching for something, or maybe both. I just knew it was time to change.

The next move in 1997 landed us in rural North Dakota. As general manager for an eight-million-dollar startup operation, I was able to draw on my construction experience. The first year was both challenging and rewarding. The second year was a management nightmare. Uncontrollable conditions with weather made everything I knew about pig production seem irrelevant. The crew and community were comprised of hard drinking, hardworking good old boys and girls. I didn't fit in. Their routine was to go to the local bar after work. If they weren't working, they were in the bar or passed out somewhere. Everything seemed to revolve around alcohol. I simply didn't participate. If you're the one sober person in a room full of drunks, it's not a fun time. I was just not into it. There were also some politics in play with management. I was never accepted as one of the group, and over time I became ostracized. The tension grew and I was near the end of my three-year cycle, so I left North Dakota in 1999.

The next job in Minnesota lasted until 2006.

We stayed longer in Minnesota because the kids were in their teens, established in school, and (frankly speaking) Marsha put her foot down. I ended the Minnesota job by choice. I was still restless. And now the kids were grown and out of the house. Marsh and I were officially "empty nesters." You must remember, at this point we had been together for over two decades. We had been raising children for the entire time. This was our first sense of freedom, and I had nothing keeping me there.

Since leaving Michigan in 1991 and leaving Minnesota in 2006, I still rarely kept in touch with the family I had left behind in my home state. It was my way of dealing with the pain of my past. I would call Mary on Christmas, Mother's Day, and her birthday. It was the minimum of respect I was able to show her, and for the sole reason that she had given birth to me. Nothing more. I was sober but restless. I had buried my childhood so deep I couldn't even remember what it was like.

As I have grown older, I have become acutely aware of relationships between a son and his father or mother. As I reflected on the dynamic of those relationships that I witnessed in other people over the years, I realized that it was not the same for me. I didn't have a normal relationship with either of my parents. I was bitter about that for a long time. I should be happy for those people. I would never want anyone to experience what I did with my parents. But it did sting when I heard stories about one of my buddies going to a ball game or hitting the casino with their dad. Fond childhood memories of fishing or hunting.

Occasionally, in the present, I will be asked about my own experience. My response is, "My old man was a monster. The world is better off without him. That's all I've got to say about that." My challenging childhood and the lack of connection with my father has motivated me to be a better father and role model. I summoned the courage to break the cycle. I am proud of that.

A dream is just a goal without a date stamp. Before I moved to Seattle, I always had a vision of living near mountains with evergreen trees. I had a postcard photo of a mountain scene with snowcapped peaks and fir trees taped to my office wall. I have no idea how I got it. Long before I got this postcard I would doodle while working. I always sketched a mountain scene with evergreens and birds in the sky with a beautiful beaming sun. When I graduated high school, I bought a Chevy truck, and it had a huge, expansive mountain scene on the rear window of the cab. I had never even seen those mountains in person, but still they called to me. It was such a strong vision that before my first trip to the Pacific Northwest, I got a tattoo with the same mountain scene I had sketched a million times even though living in that kind of world was nothing more than a dream.

I eventually found that dream in Seattle and the surrounding Puget Sound area.

In 2000 we took a family road trip to Seattle. It was a graduation present for our middle son. He was really into grunge rock and wanted to see the scene where it all began. We drove from Minnesota to Seattle along Hwy 2, also known as the Highline Road. We didn't even have a destination other than to find Kurt Cobain's house. We came to Seattle from the north. I remember the first moments seeing the mountain ranges as we came in. It was extraordinary. When we arrived, I knew this was where I wanted to live. This was the destination I had been looking for: the scenery, the diverse culture, the feeling. I didn't feel like an outcast. I felt at home.

While exploring Seattle—camping and hiking all the way to the Pacific Ocean—I told Marsha that I could live there. I had a sense of inner peace I had never known before. She liked Seattle as well but firmly told me no more moves until we were empty nesters. I understood and set my goal to work towards a new adventure. I had no idea what I would do for a living, but I knew I had to move there.

After the trip we went back to our home in Minnesota, but I hungered to relocate. I had countless conversations with Marsha but ultimately, we decided it was best to stay and let our youngest son finish high school in the Midwest. He was well established in school, sports, and the community.

Just to make sure I had not been stuck in a honeymoon trip, Marsha and I traveled to Seattle again in 2003. I fell in love all over again. While driving back to the Minnesota, I literally cried. I did not want to go back to our life. I had made a commitment to my family to stick it out until the kids graduated from high school. But I did set a date to move: June of 2006. My dream had now become a goal. Every action from then on was focused on moving to the West Coast.

I knew I wanted to be in a thriving city with plenty of employment opportunities. I was ready for a change! I took classes online to obtain an IT degree with the hope of improving my job opportunities. I studied my ass off while holding down a physically demanding, sixty-hour work week at my job in agriculture. I lived on four hours of sleep. But I was driven! I was hungry and I wanted a real change. Once again my childhood abuse was giving me the tools I needed to be successful: tenacity, focus, and the ability to compartmentalize. It didn't hurt that my relationship with my boss was tense. That bitterness helped drive me. I guess I was proving to myself that I was better than that…just like I had risen from the carnage of my childhood.

For most of our time between Michigan and Seattle—around fifteen years—I compartmentalized my past. I was vaguely aware of some things. If someone close to me had asked me if I had ever been abused, I would have acknowledged the physical and verbal abuse from both my parents. The feelings around them were hidden but I had an awareness of them. The sexual abuse was another story. That was buried deep under hard rock, and I was in no way ready to deal with it yet. I was focused on work, focused on raising my family. The rage that would emerge with a fury later was still under many layers of pain that had not yet been peeled back.

The adrenaline drive that had helped me cope as a child was also a sleeping dragon. Other than some social bike riding with Marsha and borrowing my son's bike to ride to work in Minnesota, I had not yet been lured into the competitive cycling that would later become part of my coping (and eventually healing). The only physical push I gave myself was to start exercising daily when I feared I would start resembling the old man. I did not want to be the soft fuck that he was. My six-foot frame was carrying 200 pounds of softness. I had a forty-inch waist and skinny arms and legs.

One day I went deer hunting with my youngest son out on some rough terrain in northern Minnesota. He seemed to manage the ridges and hills with ease while I was huffing and puffing, nearly crawling. That was it. I was soft. I bought some home equipment and started exercising every day. It is that same drive that would lead me to biking after we settled in Seattle.

Just before we left Minnesota, we held my youngest son's high school graduation party. I had been sober now for 15 years, ever since we left Michigan in 1991. I had not consumed a drop of alcohol in all that time. I had maintained my sobriety by not dealing with my past. I put it in a box and shoved it to the furthest corner of my mind. I detached. It was a great tool for a short period of time but was destined to fail on the long-term plan.

At the high school graduation party, I had a drink with my son. It was something we had never done before. He had joined the Amy and would be heading to basic training in a week. I knew he was going into harm's way and that I may never see him again. I wanted to have that memory. This was just a few years after the 9/11 bombings. I had one son already deployed in Iraq and another one about to get into the mix. If you have never sent a child into harm's way, then you cannot comprehend. Did I know I was taking a risk with the drink? Yes. Was I worried that it would consume my life and throw me into the death grip of addiction? Absolutely not. I hadn't thought it through that much. I had a false sense of security. The environment I was in at the time—a graduation party—didn't help. There were kegs galore and hard liquor, and I was probably the only one not drinking from the get-go. That didn't make it right, but it did make it easier to make poor choices.

The first drink I had in over fifteen years was a hard lemonade. I couldn't even finish it. It was bitter and burned my throat. Marsha gave me a look of shock when I opened the bottle. She looked me in the eye and said, "Are you sure?" I told her, "Yes, I can handle it" but the truth is, I wasn't sure I could handle it.

Turns out, I was right. This one drink was the beginning of a slide down the slippery slope of addiction. The wicked mistress had loosened her death grip, but now the hand was starting to tighten once again.

The week after our youngest son went off to basic training, Marsha and I packed everything we owned into a semi and moved across the United States to Tacoma, WA. We put our belongings into a storage unit. We had no home, no job, no prospect of employment. We took a big risk. I didn't like the life I was living in Minnesota. I knew I had to change. I was working at a dead-end job. I had reached the peak of my career in agriculture. Even a different company or location would not offer me new challenges and opportunities. I was burned out on agriculture. I walked away from a good paying job with stability. I knew I had to take a risk to find a better future.

We stayed in our camper and with our oldest son who was stationed at what was then McChord Air Force Base near Tacoma. We literally lived out of a suitcase and traveled around the Puget Sound area until our youngest son graduated Army Basic Training in August 2006 from Ft. Jackson, South Carolina. We attended his graduation ceremony. To see all those soldiers walking and knowing my son had done that hard work and dedicated himself to his country like his older brother had…that was deep. It was the proudest moment in my life as a father.

I had not taken one drink since my son's high school graduation a couple months earlier. I was still under the illusion that my drinking was still under control. But I was wrong. Marsha and I were now empty nesters and also making a huge change in our lives. The atmosphere was ripe for those old memories and feelings to start to surface, and it wasn't long before they did with a vengeance.

SPOKES

When a former millionaire was asked "How did you go broke?" his answer was simple "A little at a time and then all at once." It's the same for the addict. When asked "How did you become an alcoholic?" My answer is, "I never woke up one day and just decided to live the life of addiction. It happened a little at a time and then all at once."

When you finally get sobriety right, it is very empowering. Mental clarity comes back over time. At some point I began to recognize that my relationship with alcohol was self-destructive. When I was in the throes of addiction, I thought I was invincible. In reality, I was just lucky to be alive and beat the odds.

CHAPTER SEVEN
BRAZIL AND THE BACKWARD SLIDE

Life is short; shorter for some than others. Each day is a clean page. Write your own story. Each day is a new opportunity for success. Events of the past should not dictate your future.

Two days after the basic training graduation, Marsha and I boarded a plane for Brazil. When I was working in Minnesota as manager over several farms, we employed young men and women from other countries who came to work for us to learn the craft of large-scale pig farming. It was on-the-job training for them, sort of an internship. Marsha and I had welcomed these people into our homes and wove them into the fabric of our lives. We treated them as our sons and daughters. Many of those relationships have endured the test of time. One of the groups was from Brazil. They convinced us to visit their home country so we could meet their families and experience their lifestyle. They wanted to reciprocate the kindness we had shown them.

So that's what we did.

Marsha and I traveled abroad in Brazil for three months. We lived from couch to couch, traveling from the east coast of Brazil to the border of Paraguay on the western border, averaging three days per stop. We were vagabonds traveling by bus and hitching rides from friends and friends of friends. We had so many amazing experiences.

One of the most memorable was when we traveled through the Pantanal. It is a wetland, roughly fourteen times larger than the Florida Everglades. We stayed at a remote outpost that took two days to get to traveling by car and truck, eventually leading to a narrow road that turned into an even more narrow road. The base camp was well equipped and staffed. It was a large compound complete with riding horses. It was normally a big tourist attraction, but we were the only guests there at the time. The only source of electricity was from a generator which was turned on for one hour in the morning and two hours in the evening. To this day I am in awe of the sound of silence. The wildlife was amazing! Macaws were plentiful. Parakeets seemed endless. I cannot even begin to describe the beauty of the landscape. It was flat but lush with varying shades of green. The flowers came in infinite shades of white, pink, red, purple, orange, and created an olfactory experience that would rival the finest perfume shops. There were monkeys that seemed unafraid of humans. This I believe is a direct result of decades with no hunting. They had no reason to fear humans. They would stop and observe us like we were the ones on display.

While horseback riding in the Pantanal we rode through a small group of caimans, which are a smaller version of alligators. They reach a length of six feet when fully grown. The guide told us to keep calm as the horses navigated the reptiles. The horses stepped right over the caimans. How they knew how to maneuver them so precisely I will never know. We headed to a small pond and fished for dinner. Marsha and I caught what looked like a bullhead but was probably from the catfish family. The language difference sometimes made translation difficult. Our guide called them bullhead. We also caught piranha. Yes, the same kind that devour flesh. They are a very light meat and taste delicious when pan fried.

The caimans were on the other side of the pond. It didn't take long after we started catching fish for them to get curious. Or maybe they sensed the opportunity to seize a free meal. The fish we caught were lying on the bank of the pond, flopping. One of the caimans decided to eat one of the bullheads I had caught. I saw his move and grabbed my ever-present video camera. The caiman stalked to within six feet of me and leapt through the air like it was launched from a slingshot. It caught the fish midair and devoured it in seconds, bones crunching to emphasize the power of its jaws. Mother nature has created some truly amazing experiences for us to enjoy. Dinner was delicious minus one fish, but the stories and memories were priceless.

I cannot say enough good things about the guides in this outfit. They were always cordial, patient, and worked tirelessly to ensure we had the amenities to keep us comfortable. Our field guide knew exactly where to position us for the best photo opportunities, yet he still kept us safe. Although I love the luxuries of civilized living, there is a part of me that is envious of their simple life unencumbered by the fast pace of today's lifestyle.

It was an amazing journey. Marsha and I grew closer than ever. As incredible as this trip was, it was also the continuation of my relapse. The drink at my son's high school graduation had opened the door. Brazil ushered me in. During this time, I had a false sense of strength with my relationship with alcohol. Alcohol had always been my first choice to numb the pain of a lost and broken childhood. Vodka was my best friend. I had a flask engraved with *Loco Polocko*. My Brazilian friends called me this because I was the crazy Polish guy with a high tolerance for the cold weather. When we were together in Minnesota, where winters are brutal, I would be walking around in jeans and a t-shirt when it was twenty degrees Fahrenheit with snow on the ground. The Brazilians would be bundled up and still shivering.

As our Brazilian adventure continued, I became more comfortable with drinking. One drink led to another, and then led to shots. I gained a false sense of control over alcohol; the illusion that I could be a social drinker. Nothing could have been further from the truth. Partying is a national past time in Brazil. They celebrate everything, usually in excess, and you can only say "No" so many times. As we traveled abroad and met friends and their families it was always cause for celebration. The *caipirinhas* is Brazil's national cocktail. It is made from cachaça—sugarcane hard liquor—with sugar and lime added. This drink would come out frequently, and the night would end early in the morning. I was able to keep up the facade of having control over my addiction, mostly because partying in a foreign country can end badly if you get blackout drunk. While I managed to avoid any trouble, I had little control over the compulsion.

I thought I was invincible. But upon my return to the States, I realized I was broken inside. I finally decided to acknowledge the demons I had been suppressing for decades. Something about drinking allowed my past to come to the surface. When I was drinking, in the moment, the thoughts remained suppressed; when I would sober up, I would ask myself why I drank, and then the memories would surface. This was just starting to evolve as we wrapped up our Brazil trip. But it was enough.

For the first time in my life, I spoke of my childhood abuse. It was November 2006, and I was lying in our makeshift bed of an air mattress with Marsha. This was the first time I had ever told anyone about what happened to me. I whispered the confession to my wife and told her that I was sexually abused by my father when I was a child and that my mother facilitated the events. The shock in her voice was intense.

I knew I had crossed a line that could never be reversed. It would take another decade before I faced those demons head on and began the healing process. I am not sure why it took a lifetime to verbalize the abuse. Maybe I had finally reached a point in my life where I needed to heal. That would take some time. I had no idea how ill-prepared I was to face my demons and process the pain.

I was scared, broken, and ready to face my past. It was never easy; I just got stronger. There was a sense of freedom in Brazil that I had never known before, but it was nothing compared to the freedom I would experience years later when I conquered my addiction.

SPOKES

Healing mental scars is a lot like dealing with a sliver. It's just under the surface. You can feel it, but you can't quite see it. You know the only way to heal is to dig deeper and get it out. It's the same with the painful memories. It will hurt far worse to deal with it but in the long run you will be healed. It won't fester over a long period of time until it gets infected. The pain will be gone, and you can begin to truly live your life. You can never move forward while you are living in the past.

Memories come back randomly the longer you are sober. You don't get to choose which ones return or when they return. Dealing with the past comes on its own terms. The timing isn't always ideal. But not dealing with it is not the answer.

64

CHAPTER EIGHT
THE WICKED MISTRESS OF ADDICTION

Addicts are driven by the need for the next high. They are crafty and resourceful. Never underestimate an addict's resourcefulness. They can look you in the eye and tell a lie that even they believe.

When we returned from Brazil my top priority was to find a job…any job. I needed to start the cash flow. More importantly, I needed to get back in the groove. I needed to create a daily rhythm. Our bank account was drained, and I was hungry for the next adventure. Three months without an alarm clock opens the door for complacency. I had gone to college for Information Technology (IT) development and had always planned to land a good job with one of the major players in the Pacific Northwest. I sent my resume to over eighty companies over four days. I cast a wide net hoping to land a job to generate some income and get back into the rhythm of working daily. I had interviews lined up in a steady stream. I even interviewed for a coffee roaster and armored truck driver. I wasn't particular about what I did for a living. I was happy to be living in the Pacific Northwest.

The first job that resulted in an offer was with a small company that provided property research information to real estate investors. They focused exclusively on foreclosure property sales. They also provided short term loans for purchase with no credit check or asset verification. This is known as a hard money loan. Short term, high interest rate, designed as a bridge loan. I landed an entry-level position updating their website. It was mundane work, and I really didn't plan to stay. I just needed a steady paycheck until I could get the lay of the land figured out.

However, that changed quickly. I liked the energy of the company. I saw opportunity. I worked hard and asked a lot of questions. I had a good attitude, and they didn't have a lot of rules. Within months the opportunities for learning new skills started coming. I loved every challenge. The determination of my youth was carrying me forward. I took the advice that my late father-in-law Max had given me decades before: "Work hard and learn every job in the company. It's harder to get laid off when the cuts come." It was solid advice. I learned the foundation of the business. This is where I also discovered my ADHD could be an asset. I could multi-task like a champ. Eventually a slowed economy after the 2008 banking crash brought new challenges; the slower marketplace created new opportunities for growth. I worked tirelessly and threw myself into the effort.

Life very quickly became too good to walk away from, and comfort replaced the restlessness I had previously experienced with every other job. In the process, I let my guard down and addiction encompassed every fiber of my being. I began to drink more. The drinking increased with moments of highs, lows, and rock bottoms. The wicked mistress of addiction was like a boa constrictor slowly and methodically coiling around me. I had become far too friendly with her and now I was dancing on the edge of disaster. Drinking was nearly a daily occurrence and drinking to excess was the new normal. I have never been a public drinker. I always stayed home. Maybe a few friends would stop by. I would listen to music and do shots. I rarely drank mixed drinks.

At first it was drinking for the Friday night unwind from the work week. That quickly led to round two of Saturday night drinking. As time rolled on and the addiction became more controlling, I started Wednesday night drinking. Then it was Monday night drinking to take the edge of the start of the work week. It was easy to justify a drink for any occasion. Or no occasion. After five or six shots I would feel the familiar warmth of a buzz moving through me. It was a sweet spot of pleasure that always left me craving more. Problem was, there was a small window for that feeling before it went off the cliff into a black abyss.

Funny thing about addiction. When you are at your peak of consumption you are also at your deepest, darkest point in life. It's as if you must reach maximum intake before you can hit the bottom of the pit. There is something about the high velocity of self-destruction that provides you with the strength and courage to rise up and move forward. It's horribly painful yet the success is marvelously rewarding.

A few years after the 2008 banking and real estate crash, the economy improved, and we were facing another boom. Our company was poised for hyper growth and that is exactly what we did. Despite my successful career, my substance abuse was growing. I used alcohol to mask the pain of my childhood. I didn't understand it at the time, but I would need to face my childhood demons before I could get sober for good. Somehow by the grace of God I stopped drinking before everything good in my life all came crashing down. But there were still casualties. Those closest to me—my family—were witness to the overindulgence. For others in my extended inner circle, I was a stand-up guy with a great career and family. Athletic and successful. A superhero of sorts. They didn't see the flaws that I kept hidden behind the mask of positive energy. But I was a disaster waiting to happen.

Before moving to Seattle, I had been clean and sober for fifteen years. I did it all on my own. I threw myself into my career and did my best to be a good father, husband, and provider. It seemed to work for a little while, but the demons always came back. Staying sober takes a tremendous amount of strength and determination. It also takes a lot of therapy to avoid relapse. That was the component I was missing on the west coast. I never addressed the reason "why" I was an addict. I never faced my childhood abuse or the people who did it. That is the main reason I relapsed; I never faced my demons.

During my fifteen years of sobriety after I left Michigan and until we landed in Seattle, riding a bike was not an integral part of my life. Ironically, when I started to relapse, my relationship with those two wheels started to solidify again. It's almost like the bike is a guardian angel beside me when I need it most. Riding down my driveway when I was a kid provided a rare freedom from the abuse. During the decade and a half when things were busy and life was good, I barely touched a pedal. Then, just before I started down the dark road of addiction again, the biking kicked up again. It was as if that angel were holding my hand and whispering: *This is going to get tough for a while, but I'll be here for you.*

When I was living in Minnesota with Marsha and our kids, I was riding very little, just socially with my wife. After we moved to Seattle, it wasn't long before I was mountain biking three days a week. It was something I had wanted to do for a long time, well before we took the journey to the Pacific Northwest. I had seen some videos online and it called to me. We were less than a year into our move when I bought my first mountain bike. It was very entry-level, but I rode the wheels off it for the better part of a decade. I even used it to commute to work. I'm sure I got some puzzled looks when people spotted me whizzing down the streets on a bike designed for rocks and roots. I didn't care. I was on two wheels and in those moments, life was grand.

It takes some effort to mountain bike; it's not like you just get up and go, at least not where I live. The trails are steep and narrow; the roots in the woods are exposed and can be quite rough even on the moderate trails; drop-offs can be deadly. Mountain biking in the Pacific Northwest requires focus, so even though I was drinking a lot at that time, I was also mountain biking a lot. In some ways the adrenaline high was a reprieve not only from all the stuff going on in my head (which I had not yet addressed) but from the addiction itself. That kind of freedom is awesome, and…well…I don't do anything half-assed. Pretty soon the mountain biking turned from freedom to "out of control." I was going physically fast and furious on those trails. It's risky and even dangerous at those speeds, requiring tremendous focus to pick the right line on the trail to avoid a crash. A half inch off can result in disaster.

But that's a part of the attraction, right? The faster and more intense I went, the riskier and more dangerous it was, but the more it drowned out the noise of my addiction.

I suppose the rush from mountain biking distracted a bit from thinking about my childhood abuse. But more so, it provided freedom from my addiction. Though it was fleeting, while I was out there flying on two wheels, I was in control. I was free from it all, just for a little while. I was in nature, I could smell the earth and the leaves, I could feel the wind on my face. Even at the high speed I attained, I had peace.

I don't know whether it was a furious need to have that control, or some other drive or escape, but I rode the mountain trails extremely hard. And I fell on those trails even harder. In 2010 I had a major crash which might have been the beginning of the end of my mountain biking career. I'm lucky I walked away from it mostly intact. In fact, I'm lucky I walked away at all.

I have always loved the Tiger Mountain trail, which is a fifteen-mile out-and-back path in the Cascade Mountain Range foothills about thirty-five miles east of Seattle. The long fire road snakes up the mountain with varying intensity, spiking the heart rate when the grade hits twenty percent. It is an artful balance to get up out of the saddle for the power required to make the climb and still get enough grip from the rear wheel to avoid a spin out and loss of momentum (which means getting off the bike and finishing that section in "the walk of shame"). Push the limits hard enough and you will be gassed at the summit or puking or both. What a beautiful way to turn myself inside out! Welcome to the pain cave.

I went up to the mountain one day with George, a guy I rode with on occasion. He was a tenacious Pole like me and twenty years younger. We competed with each other all the time. George was better on the descents, but he also had better equipment. The single track back down the mountain made all the pain and suffering well worth it. The switchbacks and drops provided all the technical maneuvering I could ask for. The straight, gradual descents between the switchbacks brought a huge burst of speed and I could use my technical handling skills to avoid the roots and rocks. Picking a smooth line required intense focus.

On one steeper section of a straight descent there were a series of small drops. I could really gain some speed and hop off them, which would launch me into the air giving me the sense that I was flying. About two thirds of the way down this segment I lacked enough air to stick a landing. My front wheel caught a root and sent me over the handlebars in perfect missile fashion. I remember seeing the stem coming directly at my face. I tucked my chin into my chest and rolled with the bike. The stem hit me squarely in the chest with a THUD. At the same time, the bike smacked into the ground. Everything went black and I woke up some time later, tangled with the bike, not breathing, and numb from my waist down. I was so entangled up with the bike I could not tell where I ended and where the bike began.

I fought the urge to panic when I realized I wasn't breathing. The thought crossed my mind that I might not make it out of this one. But this was not my first crash. I focused on relaxing as I knew that would be the first step in getting my breath back again. I managed to accomplish that in what seemed like an eternity but was probably no more than half a minute. The next step was to take physical inventory. I could still move my arms and didn't see any blood. I didn't have any excruciating pain, but I also couldn't feel the lower half of my body. I was still tangled up in the bike. I concentrated on relaxing and tried to wiggle my toes. Nothing. So, I just kept focusing on feeling my lower body. After what seemed like a couple minutes my toes started to tingle. Progress!

The feeling gradually worked its way up my legs until I could feel them again. I then worked on getting unsnarled from the bike. Once I had untangled myself, I half-crawled/half-dragged my broken body over to the edge of the trail and propped myself against a tree. My legs were too weak to walk. I took inventory of my body again. Still no blood or sharp pain. When you are in survival mode, time is meaningless. The seconds tick by agonizingly slow. Your brain is racing, trying to assess every micro-message the body is sending. The minutes feel like hours and you have no clue how long it took to play out unless you have a watch. I did not and it really didn't matter in the end.

Another rider came down the mountain. He stopped and asked me if I was all right. I told him yeah, just pulling myself together and asked him if there was any blood. He had a scared look on his face and confirmed that there was no blood but said I didn't look good. He asked if I needed help. I didn't think to tell this guy that I wasn't exactly a picture of beauty when I started this ride. WTF? Don't look good? What is this, a fashion show? He was just being polite, but I was hyper-focused on sorting myself out. I was less concerned with how I looked and more wondering if I was going to be able to ride again. The guy went on down the mountain and I finished pulling myself back together. Once I was able to get myself up, I put the chain on my bike, which was otherwise fine. George did circle back just as I was getting on the bike. I rode back down the mountain at a very slow pace to the car. Packed up my gear and drove home.

When I got home, Marsha asked me how the ride was. I told her fine; had a little spill but nothing major. I showered and took another, closer inventory. Amazingly, I wasn't even scuffed up. My chest hurt where the stem smacked me, and it bruised the next day. Aside from that, I was fine. Nothing to see here folks. Move along.

Several days later I was talking to a guy I knew and shared my story. He is a seasoned Iron Man competitor who is no stranger to injuries. He told me "You got your bell rung; better get it checked out." I ended up taking his advice, reluctantly. I had been hearing ringing in my ears for the past three days and my brain was foggy and hazy. I knew I should get the professionals involved, so I made a doctor appointment. After telling my general practitioner the story—the WHOLE story—he gave me a lecture about stopping riding altogether or at least, only riding at a social level. I gave him the standard bobblehead yes so that we could both move on. This brought on another MRI and an appointment with a concussion specialist who worked with the Seattle Seahawks. If this guy couldn't fix me, there was no hope. All the tests came back fine but there were multiple conversations about injuries, their cumulative effect, quality of life, and death.

I knew I had to dial it back a notch if I expected to live a life worth living. Being a non-functioning mass of flesh wasn't a good look. So I sold my mountain bike...and of course I bought another. The new one was far more technically advanced. It had a much better suspension and bigger tires to roll over the roots and rocks. It took the drops much smoother thanks to the full suspension.

I guess I should have learned my lesson from Tiger Mountain, but I continued to ride the hard trails for several more years. In 2012 my addiction and that need for freedom met in another hard crash that marked the end of my mountain biking days.

It was September and I was riding on a local trail near my house. I had logged countless hours on this one, the Big Finn Hill trail. I had that to my advantage. Not to my advantage was that I was coming off a night of blackout drinking, which was normal for me at the time. I felt good, but in retrospect I realize my reaction time was lagging. I was in the depths of alcoholism yet still fully functional on a daily level. Or at least, functional enough to fake my way through the day and a demanding career. Now that the fog of addiction has cleared, I recognize that I could have been so much better if I was sober. That's the thing about addiction; it robs you of potential. Even if you are good as a functioning addict, you could be so much better if you were clean. Unfortunately, it took me many more years to recognize that cold, hard fact.

On the trail I came through a corner that I knew well, cutting it as close to the underbrush as I could without getting shredded by the berry bushes. I didn't want to slow down, so I was working against the natural tendency to scrub off speed on that tight of a turn. My right fork hooked a large tree branch sticking out and stopped my forward momentum instantly. I was launched over the handlebars and body-slammed to the ground. It's amazing how a half inch off your line can result in an epic failure. My helmet saved my life, but I was knocked unconscious. I woke up some time later and assessed the damage. No blood or broken bones. The bike is fine.

I knew I had taken a serious hit. At that point I was wearing a full-face helmet that revealed all my previous crashes in its many scuffs, scrapes, and dings. I had put a date on each mark after the event. The helmet was a stark reminder of how many head bangs I had taken over the years. Over the next week I had all the classic concussion symptoms. Foggy brain, tired, headache. I knew what I had to do. No need to visit the doctor for the same treatment protocol I had received forty years earlier with my first concussion and many times since. I knew the drill: Get into a dark room, avoid lighting, no visual or audio stimulation, no electronic devices. Just sit in a dark room, don't go to sleep, and let my mind fill my head with all the dark thoughts it can create. Or I could take control of the situation and react to it in a positive way to begin my healing process.

It took a few weeks of deep soul searching before I accepted the reality of several things. First, I had to get sober. It would take another three years before I got serious about that. Second, I had to either stop mountain biking or slow down. After much reflection I decided to stop. I thought a lot about my riding style. Always pushing the limit of speed and skill. I knew I didn't have a half-throttle, only full speed ahead. It was pointless to try and reprogram the man in the mirror to take a more leisurely approach to this activity. That was a no-win conversation with myself. I was constantly looking for bigger rides, bigger drops, more speed, and more risk. The outcome was predetermined if I continued. At best, I could look forward to an accumulation of injuries and a lot of good stories. At worst, the injuries might leave me with a cognitive impairment that prevented me from sharing the ride of a lifetime with anyone who would listen.

It was hard for me to accept that I was getting older. I didn't bounce back from injuries like the days of my youth. I accepted that I would get old, but I could not accept getting soft. Giving up mountain biking was the first step towards getting soft. To keep the passion alive, I decided to focus more on road riding. I never looked back.

I've been blessed with the gift of countless epic rides over varied terrain. From the flowing effortless slick rock of Moab to the forests of the Pacific Northwest to the deserts of Arizona, I have ridden them all right to the edge. I am grateful for the opportunities.

Eventually, I made the decision to sell my mountain bike. There was no doubt in my mind that it was the right thing to do. It was what I needed to do. By this time, after multiple crashes and concussions, I was risking that the next crash would be my last. The bike had to go; it was the only way to guarantee I wouldn't go back. The bike wasn't that old, I'd only had it for a year. Full suspension, all the latest and greatest upgrades, and I had bought it brand new. It was badass, no physical limitations unlike my previous bike. It allowed me to go faster, which allowed me to crash harder. The good and the bad. I put this bad boy up for sale online and some young guy bought it. It really wasn't difficult. I had come to terms with the reality of my physical state. I had been beat up by the trails so many times and the concussions were taking a toll. The blackout drinking was also affecting my brain, and not in a good way. It was time.

As the mountain biking days were winding down, I ended up racing triathlons with coworkers. What started out as a fun idea quickly evolved into competition unlike any I had ever experienced. A woman I worked with was a runner, so we put together a bike-swim-run team. I did the bike leg, and it was very therapeutic for me…*while I was competing.* I had to stay hyper-focused on training, because as we have established, "half-assed" is not in my vocabulary. I must go all in. And for me, that means, I must win or turn myself inside out trying.

I loved the triathlon atmosphere, and I loved chasing others more fit than I was. My lack of fitness and the target race dates helped to motivate me to stay sober temporarily and train harder. It would work for short periods of time during the race season but in the off season I was rapidly back to my old habits of drinking to blackout. The people I raced with were every bit as competitive as me, so it was a good fit. We also shared the battle of addiction, which made it easier to hold each other accountable.

One of my teammates was also a recovering alcoholic battling their own addiction. There was this strange dichotomy, this yo-yo of addiction and focus. When we were in race season, we were extremely focused, and it was beautiful. And then after the last race of the season, we'd both go off the rails and drink to blackout. It went like this, back and forth, over and over.

Unfortunately, my triathlon days were just a short stint on the road to sobriety. I had not faced the demons that made me turn to the bottle as a mask for the internal pain that I lived with every day. The team eventually dissolved on good terms. We just grew in different directions. Racing triathlons was a lot of fun and provided a good intro into road riding, which quickly became my replacement for mountain biking.

Once the focus of the triathlon ended, I started road riding a bit. But my alcoholism was getting in the way. Road biking the way I do it is extremely physically demanding. I couldn't just go and party the night before and then get on the bike and perform. There's also a mental focus needed for this type of cycling. When you're riding in a paceline—a group of riders in a row—your front wheel is maybe two inches away from the rear wheel of the rider in front of you. We're drafting and it's all for efficiency. You need an extreme mental focus of what's going on in front of you. And not *just* the bike in front of you, but the next four or five bikes in front of you. Every move comes through the paceline like a wave, so if the first rider has to make an adjustment, it comes through the rest of the paceline like a ripple. If the rider isn't acutely aware, they're probably going to crash. If you're in the back, you have to react in a heartbeat to whatever comes back your way. When you're in the front, your actions could endanger everyone behind you. I wasn't mentally as sharp as I needed to be.

And then of course there's the physical side. When you're doing intense cardio and drinking, that shit doesn't go together. You must have complete trust in yourself, your physical and your mental focus. If you don't…then you're not there. That's messing now with your trust in yourself. This was a critical piece of my decision to finally get sober.

As the days wore on and turned into months and years, the alcohol began to take its toll on my body, both internally and externally. My tolerance for alcohol had built up to a point where it was literally poisoning my body. I started to develop bags under my eyes. That old line "the bags don't match the shoes" was true. I would sneak makeup from my wife to cover up the shadows. I used eyedrops daily to mask the bloodshot eyes. I always thought if I *looked* good on the outside, I could make myself *feel* good on the inside. You've heard it before: "Fake it until you make it" or "Act as if." They all sound good, but they are just more lies for an addict to use.

It was more than just physically feeling good or bad. I needed to heal my emotional state more than anything. I had convinced myself I could be a social drinker. I did not realize that addicts cannot do that. It just isn't possible to have one or two drinks and walk away. When I hit rock bottom, I was drinking four fifths of vodka a week. Not four-fifths of a bottle. *Four bottles of a fifth of vodka.* I would blackout drink two or three times a week. I never missed a day of work or a day at the gym. I rarely had a hangover. I hid it so well, nobody knew. I had bottles hidden all over the house and garage. I would use a decoy bottle that Marsha was aware of. I would mentally mark the bottle before starting my drinking binge and refill it with vodka from a hidden bottle to make it look as if I had only drunk half of what I had actually consumed.

Because of my high tolerance for alcohol, I could drink eight shots before the effects became outwardly apparent. A fifth of vodka is approximately twenty-five ounces. When you drink eight or ten shots a day it only takes a couple of days to empty a bottle. When I was blackout drinking, I was consuming a half a fifth of vodka at a time. The more I drank, the more it took to find that sweet spot of pleasure which always quickly led to overindulgence.

To be fair to Marsha, I must say that she did have an inkling as to my level of consumption but her love for me was stronger than her need to confront me about my addiction. It was easier to look the other way and not discuss the elephant in the room. Love will make the flaws seem less significant.

That's what addicts do; they are masters at deceit. After a decade of indulging to excess, of promising Marsha and myself that I would never take another drink, I would always relapse. Sometimes I could go thirty days without drinking but then I would be right back to my old ways. I finally got tired of waking up every morning and facing myself in the mirror, knowing that I had let myself down again because I blackout drank the night before. I was tired of checking my phone to see if I had drunk texted or called anyone. I was tired of not remembering when I went to bed and what I said to Marsha. I was tired of going to the grocery store on my way home from work, grabbing a few food items, paying for them with the debit card, and getting cash back only to immediately circle back to the liquor aisle and grab a fifth of vodka. I always paid cash for the vodka because cash is not traceable. I was tired of hiding the bottle throughout the house and refilling the one bottle Marsha knew about with water or vodka from a stash bottle, so she didn't know exactly how much I drank the night before. I was tired of all the lies and deceit.

Something changed in the way I was thinking. I was finally ready to face my past and get sober. I had reached my breaking point. The pressures and demands of the job of maintaining the alcoholic were more than I could bear. It takes a lot of energy and effort to be a functioning alcoholic. Remembering my childhood took me to the edge. Hiding behind the bottle took too much energy and was no longer an option. I made a commitment to myself to get sober. I faced the shame of my past. I did it for me, not for anyone else. This was a significant turning point in my life. A defining moment. It would prove to be the most difficult thing I have ever done, but also the most rewarding.

People frequently ask me "What brought you to that decision? What happened?" Some of them just want to see the train wreck. My honest response? Nothing. Nothing that had not happened before. There really wasn't a defining moment. I just grew tired of waking up every morning knowing I was lying to everyone in my life about my alcohol consumption. I had this general sense of malaise hanging over me from the excess drinking. I wasn't hungover; I just felt lethargic. I was sick and tired of feeling sick and tired. I had a good life. A great career. A loving wife. A long marriage. Great kids. A nice house. A nice car. Nice toys. Alcohol was the one thing that could end it all. I was one blackout drinking event from the train wreck. I truly wanted to shed the weight of the shame that I carried for over forty years of my childhood sexual abuse.

It was time to get sober and get healed.

SPOKES

If you want to succeed at anything in life, you need to be passionate about your endeavors. If you want to get sober and stay sober, you must bring a high level of effort. You can't just go through the motions, read the literature, attend the meetings, and expect success. You must be passionate in your efforts! It's all on you. There is no way to buy passion. No one can gift it to you. It is something you have to develop and commit to using. It will set you apart from your peers and competitors. Passion combined with hard work will win against all odds.

I can't do anything halfway. For all of the good habits and all of the bad ones, I have done nothing "a little bit." I can say that with confidence. As I have grown older and faced my demons, I recognize and accept that I go all-in all the time. For the good things in life, this can be a useful tool for success. For the bad habits it can make winning impossible. The longer you are sober, the easier it is to see the potential for bad habits which lead to overindulgence which leads to addiction.

It never gets easy; you just get stronger.

CHAPTER NINE
I AM SOBER

Healing ebbs and flows. It isn't something you have control over. It takes time. You cannot rush it or force it. The healing must be organic. The best you can do is create an environment that will foster that healing.

I knew I was emotionally broken and scarred. I had no idea how bad it was. I had been running from my past for my entire life. The alcohol and drugs had been a convenient way to hide from the shame and the pain.

As a man, it was excruciatingly painful to admit to myself that I had been the sexual object of an adult male who was also my father. The man who was supposed to protect me and shelter me was the one who brought on the most pain in my life. The woman who was supposed to nurture and protect me was a facilitator for this ritual of pain and torture and carried out her own abuse. I could not reconcile either of these thoughts. It was heavy. There are days when it still is, but I have now accepted that I cannot change the past. I can never know what drove them to these unspeakable acts.

I took far too long to seek help. I finally got to a point in life where I could not bear the shame any longer. It was time to heal and for the first time in my life I admitted that I needed consult the professionals. That was the easy part. Facing my past would prove to be the most difficult battle I had ever won. Ever.

Less than a month after my first day of sobriety and well before I started formal therapy, my nephew Joe died unexpectedly. Because we had been so close in age, we were more like brothers than uncle and nephew. Joe meant a lot to me, that's all I can say. His dad (my brother Raymond) had died when Joe was not yet five years old. My own father didn't deserve the title. In some way, we both spent those early years without dads, and maybe that was part of our bond. I'm not sure, but I know the loss is deep.

The late great Raymond Joseph Wesolowski, a.k.a. Abdul-Aziz Wesolowski lived by the mantra "Each one, teach one." He was always a great athlete. We drifted apart after he joined the Marines right out of high school. When he completed his four years, he returned to Michigan and stopped in a few times. I was in my mid-twenties and at the height of my drinking and drug use. I wasn't the most fun to hang out with. Our childhood friendship had changed thanks to my addiction. But as the years wore on, we stayed in touch.

Joe competed in powerlifting and strong man competition across North America (under the name Abdul) while holding down a full-time job with Ford Motor Company. He rose up through the ranks at Ford and made a good life. He never had any children. He always loved the ladies and was never shy about flirting. Joe was an imposing man of huge physical stature, and his heart was as big as his chest. He would always stop to help someone he felt was in need.

Joe studied and joined the Islamic faith after he completed his time in the Marines. He would follow it throughout his life. His conversion caused a little rift in the family for a time. My mother, born Catholic and a devout Christian in spite of her abusive actions, was not happy about her nephew being Muslim. She did not keep her disappointment under wraps. Even though my history with her was tainted, her opinions still held some weight and I'm sure contributed to my lack of understanding. As the years passed, and certainly now, I realize how unnecessary all of it was. I didn't understand it then, and that's on me. I loved him, and that is all that matters.

As I grew older and regained composure, Joe and I grew closer. I still battled addiction every day. Joe was always supportive of my quest for sobriety. When I would talk to him about getting sober or my struggles to stay sober, he would always tell me, "You gotta leave the sauce alone and use more *kush*." *Kush* was his term for marijuana. During one of my first trips to Los Angeles, he texted me and said, "Go see the *kush* doctor" and he gave me the address. Because I didn't want to jeopardize my lungs for racing, I never took that advice. But I did eventually learn to "leave the vodka on the shelf." Joe never judged…he always supported, but he never enabled. That is a balance that only wisdom can bring.

As my racing career progressed, I sought advice from Joe about how to get stronger legs. He was a great mentor. I would send him videos of my squats, dead lifts, and trap bar dead lifts. He would critique them, which not only made me stronger…it kept me from getting injured. Like many things in life, good form keeps you safe and healthy. It's all about the form; strength will come with time. Joe introduced me to the trap bar, which is a bar with an opening in the center that allows you to stand in the middle. There is strain on your back and shoulders, and it is easier to build power. Few people use it. Even fewer people know how to use it correctly. The first time I tried it, my glutes were on fire. The next day Joe found it humorous and asked me, "Why you walking all funny?"

Joe always had a good sense of humor and smiled every day. I never saw him have a bad day. He never missed Marsha's birthday. Regardless of where life took him, he always texted her with birthday wishes. Joe always gave more than he took. To this day each time I step into the trap bar I look to the Heavens and give him a knowing smile. He is there constantly critiquing my form. And when I am sore, his words ring in my head: *"Why you walking all funny?"* He shared his craft with so many and never asked for anything in return.

Joe meant a lot to me. I never articulated that to him, I never verbalized it. I have a lot of remorse for that. As a result, I now make sure to tell the people I care about how much they mean to me. Maybe it will help fill that gap. When he left this world, it left a huge hole. The morning that I got the sad news from my sister, I had been thinking about him a lot. I was going to text him, but I got busy at work, and I didn't do it. That was a big "FUCK." But that's the way life goes. You make choices and you have to live with them.

Someone once asked me how I didn't relapse when he died. It had been mere weeks since my last drink. The honest answer is, I don't know for sure. I didn't grieve at that time. It would take a few years before I could face the pain of that loss. I didn't mourn until I went back to Michigan a few years later in 2018 and visited his gravesite. When Joe passed, I was fully committed to facing my demons and beating my addiction. Anything else was a distraction that could derail my goals of sobriety and healing. Grieving the loss of a brother would have jeopardized those goals. Maybe I was in shock or denial or both. Maybe I was just ready to stay the path. Maybe the voice of Big Joe was in my head, encouraging me from beyond as he did in life. He was so strong, not just physically, but mentally. My brother-in-law often says, "You can see Joe in Mike so much." That is the greatest compliment.

RIP, my brother.

It took about three months of sobriety before the fog of my addiction lifted. I had a sensation of mental clarity and a sense of inner peace. It was not complete...but it was a start. The journey of healing is long and yet it is rewarding. Just when you think you are done, you realize there is more work to do and more rewards to be found. The journey to mental and emotional healing is not linear. There are many setbacks followed by triumphs. Emotional healing is unlike anything I have ever healed from in my life. It is harder than physical healing because the progress is more difficult to measure. It is not as obvious as getting stronger or faster physically. The success measurements are there, they just look different.

Towards the end of my drinking days, I had started undergoing acupuncture treatment to improve my physical ability and athleticism for biking, and to improve my recovery after races. I had the most amazing acupuncturist, "Patricia." When I decided to get sober, I started a program to deal with my cravings. I shared with Patricia where I was at that point, and where I had been. She started doing acupuncture treatments to help with the addiction recovery. The treatments were very spiritual. She had a way of bringing the evil spirits out of me. I could feel the dark, heavy weight leaving my body. I would get this dry cough in my throat and feel the negativity dissipating. It was very empowering.

After we had undergone this treatment for over a year, Patricia recommended that I see someone about my past.

"Maybe it's about time you got some therapy," she said during one of our sessions.

I respected her and valued her advice, so I accepted her referral.

I started seeing my therapist Tom shortly thereafter and it was nothing like I expected. When I returned home from my first of many therapy sessions, I curled up on my bed in the fetal position and sobbed...deeply, uncontrollably. It was at that moment that I began to realize just how broken I was. Profoundly, emotionally broken. I felt a great sense of despair, but I also knew that I could find the courage and strength to move forward. I knew that with support I would make it through the darkness.

Throughout our sessions we delved into my past and into my parents. Maybe they were mentally ill, maybe they were just deviants. I'll never know. But for the longest time, I felt that this was my fault. Maybe if I had done things differently, maybe if I had been a better kid this wouldn't have happened. What Tom helped me realize was, it wasn't my fault. He told me *it's okay*. And some days it's not okay. I still have a lot of rage to work through. Sometimes when I feel backed into a corner, those feelings come up. I am taken back to my childhood. I am not a violent person, but I want to beat the shit out of the old man, and I can't. I still have to work through that. But at least I know, I have accepted that it wasn't my fault. That's heavy. All this time I blamed myself. It wasn't me at all. It is not my weight to carry.

Unlike any physical training I had done previously, there is no manual for dealing with mental trauma. Even with constant exercise of the mind there is no way to see a physical transformation or measure any improvement as compared to an activity like cycling or lifting weights. It's easy to get disappointed with what seems like a lack of progress. The progress is there; you just can't easily measure it or quantify it. It looks different. For someone like me who is accustomed to measuring performance with numbers and tangible data, this was a hard concept to accept.

I had to learn that the success was in my everyday life. **I am sober.** I don't have the cravings to drink. I look at alcohol and my relationship with it in a much different way. I understand how alcohol has a negative impact on my life and everyone around it. Long lost memories returned. Eventually even the sensation of those long-lost events returned. That's when I knew I was truly healing and making progress. It was a breakthrough moment when I knew I was going to be okay. It was very empowering!

There is no doubt, Tom saved my life. He gave me the tools to understand why I walked down this long dark road for so long and how to process the shame and emotional pain. I was a master at ignoring all of it. I was able to compartmentalize my emotions, which didn't promote healing. I was dealing with my past by not dealing with my past. Putting it in a box and shoving it to the back corner of my mind was not a long-term solution. My alcoholism was a coping mechanism for the man in the mirror whom I faced every morning. I didn't like that man. I felt weak despite my physical stature and daily training. Once I realized I was not alone, I could begin to shed the shame.

Let's be honest here: Many men put on a macho front. A victim of childhood sexual abuse does not match the macho image. In the back of my mind, I knew there had to be other stories like mine. I didn't realize how many until my therapist gave me the statistics. I nearly fell off the couch when he told me that something like one in four adult men are survivors of childhood sexual abuse. One in four! That's twenty-five percent of the male population! Suddenly I was not alone! I was not the only one. While I would never wish this pain on anyone, I found it comforting to know that there were others who understood what I was going through. It was empowering! Until that point in my life only three people were alive that knew about my past. Suddenly it was clear I was not the only man dealing with this shame. Think about it the next time you are in a room full of people. Look around. How many men can you count? Now, think of one in four of them being victims of childhood sexual abuse. Yet this heinous act is still such a well-kept secret.

I always looked at people who went to therapy as weak. I always thought "Why can't you just 'man up' and deal with your issues?" Therapy was for wealthy rich women in Hollywood drowning in self-inflicted drama. I was so very wrong to judge those people, or anyone else. You never know what a person is dealing with inside, behind closed doors. Once I took that first step in accepting help, I could truly start to heal. Once I admitted to myself how broken I was inside and faced my biggest demons, I found true peace. The sensation is euphoric. I am blessed to have discovered this gift of enlightenment.

During one of my many therapy sessions, Tom asked me to recall a good childhood memory with my parents. I paused before answering, searching deep for anything I could. There was nothing. Sure, I remember the old man tossing me a baseball or Mary teaching me how to play jacks but there was a sense of darkness. It seemed artificial, like they were forcing themselves to stop their lives and pretend to play a game with their son. A box to check. It was never real and there was never any true connection. I knew this even then, as a child. They couldn't even fake it for ten minutes.

Sometimes therapy sessions were comfortable, while other times they were agonizing. There was a middle ground that left me feeling vulnerable. I knew I couldn't fake it; I couldn't joke my way around the topic. There was only the raw truth. I had to look it in the eye and face it down. Many times, I would walk through the door into the waiting room feeling confident and secure only to leave the session feeling weak and emotionally fragile, like a child. I struggled for some time with the roller coaster of emotions. How could I work so hard to gain so much mental strength only to have it stripped away when I faced my demons? For decades I had compartmentalized the feelings around the abuse. Bringing up those experiences in therapy left me feeling powerless and vulnerable. It was momentarily demoralizing. I quickly learned that processing these emotions was building a foundation for greater mental strength and long-term stability. By doing the hard work I was improving my chances of long-term sobriety.

As time went on, I was able to accept the emotional vulnerability and grow with it. I learned that as I felt weak, it was the same as when I pushed myself to exhaustion at the gym or on the bike. There is tremendous pain and suffering—all of which I embrace and willingly go back to repeatedly—which is followed by healing and growth. I was getting stronger...emotionally stronger. This repeated process was intermixed with highs of achieving milestones, sobriety anniversaries, inner peace, shedding the shame, and acceptance. *It never gets easy; you just get stronger.*

I accept that.

Often during my sessions with Tom, I would thank him for the gift of his therapy which allowed me to heal and recover. His response was always the same: "You are doing all the work. I am just here." I understand this truth with every positive influence in my life. Marsha, Tom, every acupuncture therapist I have ever had, my sphere of influence, the bike, and God. I have learned something from each one. They have all shared with me a priceless gift of healing. I am blessed to have access to all these people and resources.

Therapy helped me deal with all the pain of my childhood. It gave me the tools to process the pain and guilt and shame of events that I had no control over. As I healed, I realized that the therapy was not limited to formal sessions with a trained professional. It was ongoing during every second of every hour of every day. Part of it was helping others. Sharing my story with other addicts seemed to give them hope for a brighter future. Healing, therapy, and mentoring are intertwined. They rely on each other to work in unison. Therapy cannot be effective without healing; healing cannot occur without therapy; and mentoring helps both. The process never gets easy, you just get stronger. The joy of finding inner peace is so uplifting. It brings about a sense of freedom...deep, soulful inner peace and freedom.

Some of the more difficult sessions were discussing my childhood memories. While I cannot recall any happy memories related to my parents it was therapeutic to realize it was not my fault. I didn't have a choice in the matter. I was simply in that space. Acceptance provided me with the strength to heal.

As the memories returned so did the details of the abuse. Details of patterns on clothes; odors; the décor of the house. Feelings of numbness I had as a child. The lack of emotion. As I was able to process the pain, I came to realize some of the reasons for the abuse. In talking with my therapist about the daily behaviors of my parents and their history as I knew it, he suggested there was a component of mental health issues that influenced their erratic and violent behavior. I know their history as it was told to me by Mary. She lost her mother at an early age. Her father was an abusive alcoholic. They never had enough money, never had enough food. Mary and her brother relied on charity from the local women to survive. Ray left home when he was thirteen and never looked back. He was also a victim of an abusive household. None of this justifies their actions. There was never justification...simply understanding on my part. I finally understood that it was not my fault. With each healing process, as difficult as it was to recall the details of the event, I became stronger mentally. I knew that I had the strength to stay sober and never walk down that road again. That was truly empowering!

Therapy also helped me to let go of some of the hate. For many years I have carried around a tremendous resentment towards my father. Faith has helped me to heal. It is still a daily process. I do not know if I will ever fully release the rage and forgive my parents for their heinous acts. I *have* forgiven them, on some level. I have let go of that truly dark energy. But I haven't forgotten and probably never will. There are still times when I wish the old man could reappear just long enough for me to take my anger out on him. But that isn't going to happen. I have to let go and keep moving forward.

I made tremendous progress during the nearly two years I worked with Tom. For the first few months I saw him once or twice a month, then ramped up to weekly for a while, and then back down to less frequent sessions as my healing progressed and my sobriety continued. I cannot say enough about how that relatively short time with Tom helped me. Once I was able to talk through the pain—the pain I carried every day over things that I had zero control over in my past—I was able to let go of the shame and the guilt. Those were the demons driving me to seek solace in the form of alcohol. Once you free yourself from the stigma, it feels like the weight of the world has been lifted off your shoulders. I could breathe again. I learned how to trust without guarding a piece of me.

The only reason I stopped seeing Tom was because he moved some distance away which made in-person sessions unattainable. We discussed video conferencing, but I was not on board with that. I needed to be in person. I received a referral from Tom and worked with the replacement for several more months. This would have been in mid-

2019. I wasn't really making progress in the same way I did with Tom. "Bill" was a cyclist like me and very into the mind over body concept. It's not that he didn't help me move forward. He did. He gave me some resources, techniques, and reading material that allowed me to continue making progress. It was a different format and approach than with Tom and one that better served me working through it on my own.

The effects of therapy can come very slowly. It can feel like you aren't making progress when in fact, you are. You just don't see the big impacts until later. Bill gave me some very powerful tools to help my healing and continued success. His vision board and meditation were excellent tools that I still use today. His tapping therapy to redirect thoughts and emotions has also been very helpful over the years. His recommendation to read of all of Dr. Joe Dispenza's works has allowed me to achieve a greater level of success and performance.

Then the pandemic hit, and everything came to a screeching halt. I still reflect on the therapy regularly. I seriously consider and evaluate if I need it at this point in my life. The short answer is there will probably always be a need for it on some level. I have researched a few times and never really come up with any solid candidates. Like everything else in life, it always works out as it should.

SPOKES

We all have things in our lives that anchor us. They ground us; they are the foundation. Cycling has been that anchor for me. Riding a bike as a child offered me a sense of freedom I had not previously known. Now cycling is the place I go after a stressful situation or when I feel the need to be grounded. It is the anchor that allows me to recharge and grow spiritually. Along with that foundation, there is a sense of peace and freedom. I find comfort on the bike.

Cycling gives the same feeling today I first experienced as a child when I learned how to ride. That early sense of freedom came from knowing that I was no longer bound to the house where the pain was dispensed on a daily basis. Somehow, I knew the bike would allow me to escape the situation into which I was born. Cycling today gives me an escape from the everyday pressures of life: the mortgage, bills, career, relationships, deadlines, and responsibilities. The bike gives me an opportunity to feel free at a cellular level, short-lived though it may be. It's a beautiful thing how it can soothe my anxiety and relieve stress while simultaneously dispensing deep physical pain from the inside out as I give every molecule of energy and effort into the ride. The confidence I gain after a hard ride is priceless! It brings both physical and mental healing simultaneously. That is a beautiful thing.

CHAPTER TEN
TWO WHEELS AND RECOVERY

Regardless of what you are pushing for, be flexible and drift with the current. You cannot fight the current. You cannot change the course of the river or the direction of the wind. Change your perspective and it will change your direction.

When I decided to get sober and face my demons in early 2015, I had been track racing for over a year. How that came about started years before, not long after I moved to the West Coast. That was when I met Coach Paul. He is the one who ultimately suggested I get into the sport. Paul is a multi-champion in track racing on the national and world level whom I met at a Gold's Gym in a spin class. I had been going to the gym for a while when Coach Paul joined. He was a big guy, built thick and not what you might imagine as a world-class bike racer. He came in one day and sat on a bike next to me. We started talking and hit it off. Paul saw something in me that I didn't see in myself, at least not at the time. He told me, "Dude…you don't quit. You'll fucking die before you quit."

Paul and I rode next to each other in that spin class for almost a year. Over time we talked about riding and racing and family and life. I knew he had a company where he helped people get the right fit on their bike. I also knew Paul had a racing history, but we never discussed his *palmarès* (list of races a rider has won, like a racing resume). He just kind of glazed over the whole professional cycling part of his life.

Our friendship continued to grow over the years. I even helped him out with his bicycle fitting company, acting as a guinea pig for him. First, he fit my bike, which helped me greatly. I was riding at a certain level before that, but after the adjustments, my performance level increased noticeably with the same amount of effort. My comfort level on the bike over long rides improved dramatically. Riding a hundred miles in a day on a bike is very attainable if you are not in excruciating pain due to a bad fit. It's like wearing clothes that are too tight; you can get through the day, but it will be much more comfortable if the clothes fit. I continued to help Coach Paul with some of his educational classes on the weekends.

As our friendship developed, we talked a lot about biking and that's when he recommended that I try track racing. "You'll love it! You gotta try the track!" he would say. Track racing is a physically demanding sport well beyond road racing or mountain biking. It's a different beast altogether, far surpassing what I had been doing with the bike on trails or asphalt. You can be phenomenal on the mountain or the road and then have your ass handed to you on the velodrome. The track is the big daddy of them all. You're racing all-out on bikes with no brakes. Top speed in the sprints will hit thirty-five miles per hour. Even the most seasoned road racers will tell you that track racers are crazy.

Around this same time, I met another guy through a mutual friend. "Nate" was a little different, nice guy but a little out there. I found out later that he'd had one too many concussions, but at the time he was just…off. Nate raced the track and had a lot of resources for equipment, bikes, and general biking knowledge. Paul planted the seed of track racing, but it was from Nate that learned the craft. He educated me about the history of cycling going back to Europe over a hundred years ago. A lot of people ride, but not many know the long, rich history of cycling and racing.

What I learned from Nate inspired me and brought a whole other level of respect for the athletes who compete today. The major stage races in Europe ride the same routes today as they did in the early 1900s when they started. The equipment and technology are far better now than when the sport began. Yet every athlete continues to turn themselves inside out in pursuit of the leader's jersey. It is nothing short of inspiring to see the riders of today cross the finish line with glazed-over eyes, utterly exhausted from their efforts, and collapsing in a heap on the road with saliva running out of their mouth unable to even form a sentence. You can almost feel the drive and urgency they have that pushes them to get back on the bike and continue racing after a crash—bleeding and covered in road rash with broken bones or even a concussion—but never defeated. They stop racing when they are incapacitated. It seemed like a good fit for me.

Just before I hit track racing hard, I was doing charity rides every other weekend throughout spring and summer. The road riding started to overlap with the track racing. I was working full time too, and there are only so many hours in the day. Whatever type of biking you do at a competitive level, it takes a lot of focus. Especially for me, because as we have established, I can't do anything half-assed. I am all in or nothing. I was told (and I believe this), that it takes four years to make a good track racer. Four years of discipline, training, and racing before you can even start to recognize your true potential and win races on the track. And it really does.

After I got sober, the bike became another type of therapy outside of my formal sessions with Tom. I wasn't aware at the time, but I now know that the endorphin dump caused by the extreme cardio undertaken for biking is similar to the effect of alcohol when I was drinking heavily. Exercising at that level, with that intensity, provided a chemical dump that gave me the same kind of satisfaction—or release— as the alcohol did. There is a correlation between high-intensity activity and the release of chemicals from the brain. I would literally get tunnel vision when I was done with a race, and I was so spent that basic motor skills were a struggle. But it felt good.

When I was at my peak of track racing, I raced a hundred races in one season, which started in June and was over by the end of August. I was operating at almost constant maximum intensity for about three months. Everything was about racing, which probably helped to distract from all the stuff from my past that continued to try and punch its way to the front. We usually raced in the evening and the race ended around 9:00 p.m. I would wake up the next morning feeling totally spent, physically destroyed, and knackered from the night before. Yet it felt amazing. I would open my eyes and think, *Fuck yeah! I am king of the world, look at what I just did! I'm going off to work and I just kicked everybody's ass! I'm one of the oldest guys in the building and I just fucking nailed it!* The self-esteem boost and the ego trip were awesome, but probably not healthy at that dosage level in the long term.

In some ways, the intense biking and working out were other ways I dealt with my past (and still are). When you were sexually abused as I was, you can feel powerless. For men, it can be emasculating. The rush I got from biking with such focus and ferocity probably compensated for those feelings during a time when I had not yet dealt with them. It was a validation that I am powerful. *I am a man.* I didn't want to look in the mirror and see someone weak. These things were done subconsciously, deep down, so I could beat down the demons of my past even when I wasn't ready to face them. That's why I did it, and truthfully, that's probably why I still do it to some extent.

Before I got sober, biking was almost a coping mechanism. The endorphins, the adrenaline, the intense focus, all of those were a way to deal with my past, which had not yet come to the surface fully. It was almost a therapy before I even thought I needed therapy. It didn't make my demons go away, but it helped me survive until I was ready to face those demons in the here and now. I would stop drinking during racing season, sometimes for ninety days. I always went back, but the bike was the constant. And at some point, I just got tired of poisoning myself, because I was seeing what the other side of that looked like when I was drinking and trying to race. And I was hanging around track racers. Those people don't drink. You just fucking can't. Even if you want to be at the back of the peloton, you can't be a heavy partier. So, I didn't drink during the season and eventually that helped lead to my decision to get sober.

Before I quit drinking for good, the intense biking did provide me with some relief, through endorphins, the adrenaline rush, and that feeling of power. It's the same as now, so why wasn't it enough to take me over the fence from addiction to sobriety? Easy. I wasn't ready to face my past and deal with it head on. Once I did that—when I accepted my reality and made the decision to work through the pain—there was a mental switch. It's still two pedals going around and around, but now it is no longer a coping mechanism. It became, and still is, a part of my healing.

SPOKES

Each of us has 86,400 seconds in every day. What are you going to do with them? Time is a fickle measurement. It cannot be manipulated, adjusted, borrowed, stolen, gifted, or bought. Regardless of our age or status or where we grew up or how much money we have or don't have, we are all given the same amount of time each day. It's how we choose to use it that makes the difference.

Think of the Olympic athlete who just missed a gold medal by a fraction of a second. What does that fraction of a second mean to them? Now think of the prisoner serving a twenty-year sentence. What does one day mean to them? It is all time. It is all measured the same way. It is all perspective. And each precious second is impactful in some way. Time dictates every aspect of our lives from the hour-to-hour and day-to-day. We are always preparing for something or rushing to complete some task. What nobody knows is how long we have until the finish line.

I try not to dwell on all the precious time I have wasted with over-indulgence of drugs and alcohol. I cannot change the past, but I can make better choices every day. Letting go of the shame and guilt over circumstances which I had no control takes time. I can see the progress, but I do not know how much more time it will take to heal fully. Or if that will ever happen. I know that the hate I hold for those who perpetrated these heinous acts will subside over time because I choose to let it go. I do not know how long that will take or if I will ever accomplish that goal completely. I just know that I have to make good choices every day and believe that someday I can attain a deeper level of peace.

CHAPTER ELEVEN
TOOLS

As the great Babe Ruth once said, "Yesterday's home runs don't win today's games." It is also true that yesterday's tragedies don't stop today's success. Use the hard lessons of your past to build a brighter future.

Addiction takes its time to get a grip. The path is shorter for some, longer for others. For me it was always an ebb and flow. I knew I was heading down that dark road, yet I kept telling myself "I can control it" or "I will get sober this time." I had long periods of sobriety up to ninety days, but I just couldn't keep it going. I always longed to just feel better. I wanted to go through the day without the dull pain of knowing I had endured childhood sexual abuse. I felt very alone and isolated. I thought I was the only one with this experience, or at least, that there were very few others who had gone through anything similar. Over time I would learn how wrong I was. For decades it was something I could never talk about to others or to myself. I could not even face the conversation in my mind. But I grew tired of living the lie. I was tired of waking up and seeing the shell of a man every time I looked in the mirror.

February 25, 2015, was the day I started to win. Really win. It was a hard day…but a very good day. I decided to face my past, conquer the demons, and beat my addiction. *FUCK YEAH! I won! Everything else be damned!* That's where everything changed. I got sober and started living my best life. It was a lot of hard work; still is some days.

It never gets easy; you just get stronger.

Acupuncture was another tool that helped tremendously in my recovery. Opening the meridians allows energy to flow with ease. The tightness in my body dissipates. The gnawing in my gut leaves. When the pain returns, it does not last as long. I have always been interested in alternative healing practices. Years ago, I read the autobiography of retired pro NFL player Bill Romanowski called *Romo: My Life on the Edge: Living Dreams and Slaying Dragons*. Bill was a big proponent of natural healing and alternative health practices. He raved about the benefits of acupuncture for physical recovery. As a Master's Athlete (thirty-five years and older) I was always looking for an edge. Acupuncture seemed like a good option. I researched practitioners in my area and found a clinic that fit my needs.

Acupuncture has been an integral part of my journey. One of my practitioners implemented a procedure called "Zero Reset" (also known as "Point Zero"). It has proven highly effective in the recovery of heroin addicts. There are five needles placed in the inner part of each ear. This curbs the craving for the pleasure of the addiction—in my case, alcohol. I never really craved the *taste* of alcohol. What I craved was the feeling that alcohol gave me, at least before I tipped over the edge of pleasure and into compulsive overindulgence. Even after years of this treatment I am continuously amazed at how it works. I wonder who discovered that sticking five needles into the inner portion of the ear would have such a significant effect?

Another aspect of healing with acupuncture has been the mental healing. For reasons I still cannot explain, the treatment of needles in my stomach seems to bring some dark dreams to the forefront. As I said, I still have a lot of rage left in me. My dreams have no pattern and mostly make no sense. Through therapy I learned that they are very rarely literal and transferable to the life we know and live daily. There are objects and spirits that represent our world but only the dreamer can interpret their meaning. All things are relative. There are a lot of metaphors that mean something only to the dreamer.

I never see faces in my sleep world. Only figures of people. I can feel their soul. I have a knowing sense of who they are. Perhaps I am searching for an answer or a story to directly link the chaos in my dreams with the events of my life. Perhaps it is just a release valve to vent the emotional pain. Too many days have left me with graphic images of death, a feeling of darkness that engulfs the mind, a sense of chaos, and the awareness of darkness in an evil presence. Too many nights I would wake up screaming with my heart racing and my mind engulfed in fear. I would find myself confused and depressed. The darkness would hang over me like a black umbrella all day long.

In the same way that my therapist Tom helped me to understand my past, acupuncture helped me process my subconscious thoughts. I used to wake up terrified, heart racing, panicked, and disoriented. I've progressed beyond that now but still working on it. Most of the time I cannot make sense of the nightmares. Rarely do I have dreams of peace or happiness. Dreams of protecting someone, usually a child, are frequent. Perhaps that is me, that young boy who was vulnerable and could not rely on the people in his life who should have protected him. There was no one there to protect me, so I took on the burden.

As bad as the dreams are, I now have a sense of relief, release, or solace when I wake up. When the nightmares come, they are followed with a release of anger. It is as if I have been cleansed of the sins of my childhood; sins that I did not choose to commit but was forced to participate in. The dreams have helped me to understand that it is possible to break the cycle. As hard as it has been, I have succeeded. I have broken the cycle.

When the nightmares don't wake me up, the physical pain will. The abuse my body has undergone over the decades has taken its toll on my sleep comfort. My neck gets stiff and throbs in pain. Both my shoulders are damaged to the point where I find it difficult to sleep on either side. I have done a lot of physical therapy on my shoulders and neck, but they are still not fully healed. It took a lot of years for me to find the right pillow and the right bed. It was a process of elimination. Before I bought an adjustable bed, I would prop my shoulders and legs with pillows. Due to decades of weightlifting, my arms are so large and heavy they pull on my back when I am sleeping on my side. I have been able to alleviate some of the discomfort by resting my arm on a pillow rather than my side. This relieved the pressure points that would cause pain. It takes some work to get the sleep environment right, but it is worth the effort and expense.

And as we know, sleep is important to just about any recovery.

Adding to the challenge is the fact that for as long as I can remember, I have ground my teeth in my sleep. Likely this is another gift from the horrible things my parents did to me. According to the Mayo Clinic, risk factors for teeth grinding (known as bruxism) include anxiety/stress, having a competitive personality, and having night terrors. Check, check, check. After years of grinding and accidents that literally impacted my teeth, I now sleep with a night guard. I can tell when I have an exceptionally restless night because my jaw aches when I wake up. I know I am trying to grind my teeth. I will then have a vague memory of the dreams. Overall, I am sleeping better with the guard. It was something the dentists all suggested for decades. I resisted for no particular reason other than I have an ego. I am glad I finally took the advice and now my sleep is more restful. This is just another of the many tools I use to find peace in my space.

Insomnia is another one of my close friends and another impact from my childhood that affects my sleep. I go through periods of time waking up in the middle of the night with my stomach hurting so badly that I think I am having my guts pulled out. It's kind of a gnawing hunger pain but somewhat like the pain from doing sit ups to exhaustion. It's more internal than muscular. Either way, it is nearly impossible to get back to sleep. Then my mind wakes up. Once my brain is awake, sleep is nothing more than a hope for the next night. I might as well just get up and try to be productive. Most days that's not a problem. However, by three p.m. I often feel the urge to take a nap and that *can* be a dilemma.

After enduring decades of insomnia and other sleep issues, I was able to assemble a list of tools that have proven effective in improving my slumber. First and foremost is therapy. This has allowed me to face the demons of my past; to acknowledge the hurt I suffered as a child; to accept that I cannot change the abuse; to affirm that I never did anything to bring it on; and to attest that I had zero control over the situation. Another tool is the environment of the room in which I sleep. That is critical. Pitch black works best for me. I use a blackout shade and it was possibly the best investment I have ever made. I keep it quiet and turn off the electronics. Using the blue light filter on my phone and automatically activating the *do not disturb* feature also helps greatly. It all amounts to incremental improvements. Aggregate marginal gains apply to everything we do, not just training for the big race.

Thanks to a neuro-psych evaluation after my last concussion, I was diagnosed with ADHD (Attention-Deficit/Hyperactivity Disorder) and PTSD (Post-Traumatic Stress Disorder). (ADHD is also a risk factor for teeth clenching or grinding, go figure.) I always suspected I had ADHD or something similar but now I know for sure. It helped to make sense of things I experience, like my restless habits, my short attention span, and my inability to match shapes. These are traits I have had since childhood. They never diagnosed kids for these types of mental health issues when I was growing up. If you were "hyper," they just took away the sugar and forced you to sit still in your classroom chair or face the teacher's ruler on your knuckles or back of your head.

PTSD was a whole different issue. I always related PTSD to soldiers returning from war. I certainly never considered that I had experienced anything that would cause me to be reactive because of past trauma. The neuro-psych evaluation proved me wrong once again. This also connected some of the dots, like nightmares and hyper-awareness of my surroundings—sort of like street sense on steroids. I always need to be on alert for the next threat because that is how I was programmed as a child. When I am out in the world, I constantly check reflections in mirrors or windows to see what or who is around me. I am hyper-aware of whose cars are parked in the lot at my workplace. If there is a strange vehicle, I immediately start asking myself "Whose car is that? What are they doing?" The continuous onslaught of physical and verbal abuse when I was young conditioned me to trust very few people in my adult life. Every minute of every day was spent trying to read the body language and subtle movements of my parents that would alert me to an oncoming explosion of rage. A successful read of the situation might give me the extra few seconds I needed to escape or cover up and minimize the pain.

Meditation has been another great tool in my recovery. Lying awake in a dark room in the middle of the night provides a good environment for calming the breath, quieting the mind, and transcending to a peaceful place. People frequently ask me how to meditate. I am no guru. All I can tell you is to try it. Practice. For me meditation is more of a focus. When the mind wanders, I gently bring it back to the focus point. Thoughts will come into my head, but I focus on moving past them. Like anything else, the more you do it the better you get at it. Meditation is more about letting go of the issues that run through my brain rather than finding a higher state of awareness, although I feel like that will come with time and practice. Meditation has also taught me acceptance. I can't control everything that happens around me, but I can control how I react to it.

Another tool I discovered through experimentation is the use of press tack needles. They are very small-diameter needles that are only two tenths of a millimeter long, so they barely penetrate the skin. Press tack needles have been very effective. They seem to promote energy flow, which I have found beneficial. I have also discovered a few pressure points on my skull that calm me and seem to improve my sleep. Over time I have learned to use manual pressure on those points when the press tack is not readily available. The tacks have also proven a useful tool for pain management. This technique may not be for everyone and there are risks, so do the research and consult the professionals before you give it a try. I've found that if you open your mind to unconventional tactics and try enough things, you will build a collection of the right tools to help you succeed at anything.

Before using press tacking, I considered it a good night if I slept four consecutive hours and didn't wake up to a racing heart and a panic attack. Now I frequently sleep seven hours uninterrupted. If I do have dreams, the sense of fear and anxiety are absent. Whenever I tell someone that I practice self-acupuncture, they have the same reaction: *WTF? You're crazy!* I accept that. This is just another tool for my continued success on the path of sobriety and healing. It's another edge to get me through the night and into the next day on a foundation of success. I am blessed to have this gift.

People also frequently ask me "How did you decide to do press tacking?" It was simply a natural progression. I had been attending acupuncture sessions every other week for over two years. For reasons still not fully known to me, I have a very high awareness of my mind, body, and soul. Being an athlete may be part of that. In the evenings I often relax on the couch and massage my scalp to relieve the tension of the day. One day I found a spot on the left side of the back of my skull about the size of a pea that seemed to be a nerve cluster. It relaxed me when I applied pressure. I told my acupuncturist about it at my next session. He needled it and I enjoyed the most peaceful night's sleep I could remember. I knew I was on to something. We repeated this process for a few more sessions with the same results. The only problem was that the treatment would wear off before my next session. My acupuncturist would often send me home with press tacks in my legs to aid with muscle recovery. They are imbedded in a sticker about the size of a pea. When applied, they barely break the skin but provide a stimulus for the body's natural energy to travel. I found some on the internet and counted the days until they came. Four days can seem like an eternity.

That evening, I located the spot on my skull, applied the needle, and slept through the night with the most pleasant sleep I have had in decades. It was so good that I was concerned about sleeping through my alarm. Press tacks are insanely effective and economical. I have really found something here. I will continue to use them until if/when they are no longer effective. Sleep—peaceful restful sleep, and the sense of renewal that comes with it—is priceless, especially for those of us who battle sleep disorders.

During my healing journey, there were also times when I would wake up with a dry cough in my throat and what felt like the presence of a dark spirit over me. I am sure it is the old man trying to make amends. There have been many occasions during acupuncture or when dealing with nightmares that the dry cough comes from nowhere. I can feel the darkness; it tries to consume me, engulfing me in a smothering shroud of blackness and cold. But I no longer fear the presence of my past for I know I am far stronger physically, mentally, and emotionally than my perpetrators could ever hope to be. Never again will I be controlled by their presence.

Over time I have healed and become much stronger than I ever could have imagined. My history has brought with it determination, tenacity, and the ability to rise up to be a better version of myself. This healing has been made possible by my dedication to doing the hard work with the tools of therapy, acupuncture, meditation, physical exercise, spiritual exercise, and utilizing a strong support infrastructure. I cannot change the past and I cannot change the abuse I have endured, but I *can* control how I react to it.

It took many years, but a sense of calm and inner peace has settled in me. I believe this is due in part to the acupuncture, and also influenced by my sobriety. Through acupuncture I learned about Qigong. According to Wikipedia, Qigong (also known as qi gong, chi kung, chi 'ung, or chi gung) is a "system of coordinated body-posture and movement, breathing, and meditation used for the purposes of health, spirituality, and martial-arts training." I use Qigong to calm me; to bring my mind and soul into peaceful focus. It is the rhythm of the motion and the deep breathing that allow me to calm my mind and release the anger and hate for a past I cannot change. It is about acknowledging the situation, accepting it, and moving on from it. *Control what I can control.* It has made a positive impact on my inner peace, my sobriety, my strength, and my energy.

As the duration of my sobriety grew, it became clearer to me what tools were essential for continued success. It would take more than physical strength and mental strength to stay sober. I would need to be smart. This meant more than going to the gym and beating up my body with weights or riding the bike until I turned myself inside out. I had to outsmart the demons still lurking in the shadows. I had to face them with confidence…the same confidence I had built up over years of physical success. Now it was time to start racking up the mental wins.

As the months and then years passed, the nightmares still haunted me but not as frequently. The intensity was a lot to bear but I could somehow see my way through the darkness that accompanied my emotions when I woke up. With sobriety came clarity. The clarity brought strength. The strength brought confidence. The confidence brought success. There is nothing more empowering than success. Now I was not only physically strong, but I was mentally strong as well!

It doesn't matter what happens to you. What matters is how you deal with it. Growing up I had no control over the things my parents did to me. I was not physically capable of stopping the verbal, physical, and sexual abuse they afflicted on a regular basis. I was a child and not mature enough to find a way out of that situation. They had instilled a level of fear that left me powerless to escape. Many decades later as I finally gained control over my addiction, I recognized that I could not control what had happened to me and it really didn't matter. What really mattered was how I dealt with that part.

I'm not going to lie; I have not let go of all the hate for my parents and the horrific things they did. I cannot say if that day will ever come. I do know that the hate will eat me alive from the inside if I do not let it go. I work daily using a full arsenal of therapy and tools to bring me success and release myself from the grip of hate. Sometimes the rage boils to the surface. It's difficult to control. I have learned to acknowledge this emotion, move through it, and move forward. Let it go...don't dwell on the past. Live in the moment and look to the future. Make every day a better day.

Acupuncture, therapy, and meditation have given me the confidence to control those emotions and move forward with my day. What used to dominate my thoughts now barely gets a passing regard upon waking. Facing my past meant facing my demons. It is the hardest thing I have ever done.

SPOKES

The inability to trust has been a lifelong challenge for me. It is rooted deeply in my childhood. The explosive violence at the hands of my parents left me with only one option at the time: always be aware of your surroundings and be ready for fight or flight regardless of how serene the moment may seem.

When I was twelve years old, I received a hunting knife for my birthday. It was a very high-quality Buck knife, a symbol of the rite of passage from boyhood to manhood. I cherished that knife and still have it to this day. It gave me a sense of safety. I slept with it under my pillow for years. As a child I didn't know if I could fend off any evil that came to me in my sleep, but I knew I could fight hard and at a minimum make the intruder pay for his violence. That knife brought me peace. As I transitioned into a man, it was the only thing I could trust to protect me from evil. There were many times when I would wake up from a nightmare and find comfort in reaching under my pillow and finding the cold steel against my fingers. Fortunately, I never had to use it for self-defense. The knife and me were the only things I trusted.

Not all healing is physical. Not all injuries are physical. I have been broken not only physically but emotionally and mentally also. Sometimes the worst injuries are those you cannot see on an x-ray or MRI. There is no magic pill for mental health. Healing is not linear. I'm not sure that you ever completely heal from mental trauma. You can improve over time if you do the hard work. But I'm not certain that it ever fully goes away. It seems there will always be scar tissue. This reminds us that the past is real.

As I have healed, I have become more confident. My success with sobriety and counseling brought more success in my relationships and the search for inner peace. As I shed the weight of shame, I found it easier to stay sober. It was infectious. I felt like a champion! I was more engaged with my marriage. I was more attentive to the relationships with my children. In truth, I had always had that feeling; I just didn't recognize it because I was too numb from the booze and too busy running from my past. Confidence is within everyone. You just need to realize it and bring it forward. Unleash it!

CHAPTER TWELVE
BACK TO THE CRASH

Competition is good. It makes us better, compels us to strive each day to be a better version of ourselves. Compete with the person in the mirror. That's the only competition that really matters.

Some people say that Friday the thirteenth is unlucky. I disagree. Throughout my life, thirteen has brought more blessings than curses, proof that it has been a fortuitous number versus an ill-fated one. Still, some would argue that the events of Friday, May 13, 2016 underscored the day's superstitious reputation. I can only say that for me it was a gift. I was given the opportunity for a second chance at life.

It is the last race of the night in preseason racing. There are approximately twenty-four riders in the field. I roll up to the rail waiting for direction from the referee. I look down at the dozen or more riders ahead of me, then glance over my shoulder to see an equal number behind me. I have but one thought: *I hope you fuckers got your shit together tonight.* I have no idea why that thought pops into my head. I had a feeling about this race, a sort of premonition. In all the years of racing before, it had never happened. These guys were the same riders I had been competing against for the previous two years. Something just tells me this time to be hyper-aware.

We ride around easy in the neutral lap then get the gun to officially start the race as we roll through turn four, heading for the start/finish line. This is a twenty-lap points race. Points are awarded every five laps for the first four riders across the line: 5, 3, 2, and 1 for first place through fourth. Points are double for the final sprint on the final lap. The rider with the most points at the end of the race wins.

We are racing at the Jerry Baker Memorial Velodrome (JBMV) in Redmond, WA. This is my home track. It is an outdoor oval-shaped track

400 meters long with twenty-five-degree banked corners. The front and back straights have fifteen-degree banks. The banks angle up to a height of twelve feet in the corners. I had been racing strong all night, finishing in the top five in the previous two races. Coming through Lap 4 the pace is lifted, anticipating the first points lap for Lap 5. We are strung out five-plus riders in the pace line, lifting the pace through turn two. Down the back straight, the pace is lifted again. I am in fifth wheel (position/place) with a teammate to lead me out. We are now racing at approximately thirty-five miles per hour with mere inches between riders. Just as we approach turn three, the lead rider sits up. I have no idea why. Maybe he just blew up. These racing bikes have no brakes. They are direct drive and cannot coast. The only way to slow down and avoid rear-ending the rider in front of you is to ease up the pressure on the pedals and move up track onto the bank to scrub off speed.

With just 150 meters to the bell lap for points, I don't want to lose momentum. But I also don't want to stick my nose into the wind and do all the work. There are two riders up on the rail; I know them well. Either one will be a good lead out to steal some points in the sprint. I think, *if they jump, I am going with them.*

In the split second between seeing the leader sit up and assessing the other riders, I hear a sound behind me. It is the all-too-familiar screech of metal on cement. Once you hear this sound, you never forget it. I know this sound means someone has crashed behind me. Before my brain even has time to process, I am blindsided from behind and hit with tremendous force on my right shoulder blade.

The rest is a blur of out-of-body experiences, ambulances, emergency room lights, and feeling like my back has been crushed by a semi-truck. I am in the hospital for twelve hours while they sort me out. My memory of the events is fragmented and foggy. I have road rash from head to toe, dozens of stitches, broken teeth, a shoulder injury, and a severe concussion. I am messed up bad. The long-term recovery is just as bleak. The crash has cost me three teeth. The entire rebuilding process will take a year and a half. I average one dentist appointment every other week during that time.

For my head injury, there are numerous mental cognitive tests and a neuro psychiatric evaluation. The consensus is that I have a severe concussion but fortunately no brain bleeding. This is one too many. Only time will tell how I will heal and what will be the new normal. The feeling of isolation is overwhelming. I feel totally out of sync. My emotions are crazy, and my circulatory system is broken. I feel cold all the time and I want to not feel cold, but I cannot fix it. This is the worst concussion in my life. To the best of my recollection, I have had nine concussions that rendered me unconscious and another dozen less severe. Things that worked before no longer work. There is no manual for concussions. They are different for everyone and different every time.

I am sure there is a lot of talk about me quitting racing and riding, and on and on and on. The fog I am living in filters all of that out. Three days later I am back on my spin bike, pedaling at an extremely low cadence so as not to raise my pulse. Any significant increase in heart rate causes severe head pressure on the right side of my brain. But I take the risk. The rhythm of the bike and the motion of my legs bring a calmness into me that I have been craving. As ridiculous as it may sound, the only place I feel comfortable is on the bike. Lying on the couch or in bed, sitting on the couch or in a chair…I cannot tolerate any of it. I need to move my legs, just a little. I am not looking to achieve a personal best. I don't need a workout. I need to feel the motion, the freedom that has helped me cope with so much up to this point. I need to feel that emotion. So, I make the decision to go downstairs and gingerly climbed on my spin bike. My legs move slowly but at least they are moving. It feels good.

Marsha discovers me when she returns from a trip to the supermarket. I can only imagine her surprise (and the fire that ignites within her) as she finds me in the garage, pedaling away with my left eye swollen shut; bandages on my shoulder, elbow, and wrist; and scabs running down the side of my bruised and bulging face. Although my memory is foggy, I'm fairly certain she says something like, "What the FUCK are you doing? How do you think you're going to get off that thing?" To say she is livid is an understatement. If I were not so busted up, she would have grabbed me by the ear and yanked me off the bike.

I know she is right to have that response. But the bike is part of my therapy.

I get on it every day or so after that, and just sit there moving my legs. It's where I feel the most mentally comfortable, but also the most physically comfortable. The only pressure points are the soles of my feet, my palms, and my butt. Everything else is fucked up, so the spin bike is a pretty good place for me to be.

For many people, this vulnerable time would have been a breaking point. It has only been a little over a year since I have gotten sober. But I have built a solid foundation of sobriety prior to the crash and that helps me greatly. Still, I must be careful. The opioids they give me for pain relief are too tempting and I know the consequences of dancing with the wicked mistress of addiction. I ask Marsha to dispense them for a few days and then dispose of the rest and never give me any again regardless of the pain level. As fucked up and foggy as my head is, I am aware of the potential for relapse.

The long rebuilding process at the dentist is another area of concern. I am very honest about my history with addiction and emphasize that I do not want to use any gas regardless of the intensity of the pain. I manage the pain with local numbing agents and meditation. Over-the-counter acetaminophen takes the edge off. There is no way I am going back to the days of addiction. I have worked too hard to get here. I have faced my demons and got it right this time.

While in recovery I use writing as a form of therapy (which would become the first rough draft of TBS although I did not know it at the time). I always kept a journal but now I start to write my memoirs. It is painful at times but cathartic. I lean into the pain as always and find that once I embrace it, the intensity decreases. It becomes a perspective rather than a situation. I learn that I cannot rewrite my past, but I can control how I reacted to the memories and the emotions that come with it. My response determines the outcome.

It takes three years for my head to clear fully. During that time nobody really wants to talk to me about the crash. I have so many unanswered questions. Eventually I am able to piece it together. When the lead out train sat up, the peloton behind me didn't read the field fast enough and couldn't avoid crashing into me. I basically got rear ended. There were many riders who stop racing after witnessing my crash. There are a few more who never return to the track.

After the 2016 crash I can't ride outside or on a track for months. It is psychologically painful to not be out there. I battle depression intermittently. A few of my fellow riders ask me to coach them. I am honored although I don't feel that I have the right knowledge to share with them or much advice to give to them to advance their craft. I still lack self-confidence, another leftover from my childhood. Despite my reservations, I decide to give it a try. Perhaps the sharing and interaction will be therapeutic for me. It does help me heal and it gives confidence to those I work with. At the same time, I have a lot of inner conflict. I feel constantly reminded of what I cannot do. Yet I am grateful for the opportunity to share in my pupils' successes. The hope I have for my future and the success that I can achieve on the bike work their way to the forefront of my mind. There are no easy days; only days when I get a little stronger.

With racing being absent from my life there is only one thing to do: give it away so I can keep it. It is important for me to share the knowledge I have gained over the years so I can keep that expertise. If I allow it to sit dormant in my mind, it will fade away. The edge of the competition will dull and soften, eventually disappearing and becoming useless. So as the days pass, I become less focused on what I *can't* do and more focused on what I *can*. Eventually I start having regular thoughts of what I *can* do again. This brings me hope and inspiration. Somehow by helping others to be a better version of themselves, I inspire and motivate myself to become a better version of me. That is truly a beautiful thing.

Throughout my recovery from the crash of 2016, I eventually start to think about racing again. The 2017 season is approaching, and I realize a few things. First, my injuries from the previous year are still healing. My future in racing is uncertain. Everyone in my world outside of my teammates begs and pleads with me to stop racing altogether. I am not ready to quit, so I negotiate a middle ground. Second, no more mass start racing, which is what the 2016 crash race was. Only match sprints or time trials. It is now apparent that I lack self-confidence. It sounds ridiculous when I write it down. *I lack self-confidence.* I have been successful in so many aspects of my life, both on and off the track. But it is my truth. As I analyze this revelation, I realize it is just another unnecessary byproduct of my childhood. The constant beating and berating laid the foundation for a mindset of self-doubt. I know what I have to do. I must change my mindset. Whenever that self-doubt starts creeping in, I stop and tell myself all the reasons I CAN do it!

I spend most of the remainder of 2016 riding solo at a social level. The only people I ride with are Marsha and my then three-year-old grandson. I taught him how to ride when he was only two years old. He is my new riding buddy. I taught him how to ride and he taught me how to heal. I taught him how to sprint and he taught me how to laugh. There is something calming about looking at the world through the eyes of a child. All the things that cause stress seem to disappear and calmness takes over.

Later in the summer of 2016 I go back to the track for training. I have to ease into the efforts because if my heart rate gets too high it will cause tremendous pressure on the right side of my brain. I can tell I am still healing. Mentally this is a tough time for me. I still want to go, go, go. I read a lot about healing the brain and ultimately develop an arsenal of vitamins and supplements to support brain health and improve cognitive skills. I know I have a solid foundation for my cardio and strength. It is my brain I need to heal before I can consider racing again. Lifting weights does not cause the same head pressure as intense cardio, so I focus on strength training. If I don't lift too heavy, I can avoid the head pressure.

I eventually jump back_into the team rides on the road and quickly discover I am not as soft as I thought I was. I still have a strong kick to the line and an explosive sprint. My endurance is lacking but that will easily improve as I am able to increase the intensity of my training. There is only one thing I need to get back into race form and that is time. I spend a fair amount of time training with my good friend and teammate Diallo. I need a wheel I can trust, and he needs someone to push him. As we say, iron sharpens iron.

It starts on the track. The flying 200TT provides an excellent platform for this change in mindset. For years I could never turn in a time anywhere close to sub 13 seconds. The clock was my nemesis. Once I break free of the self-doubt, I not only turn in sub-13's, I smash it with a PR of 12.68 seconds. This is, for me, a huge jump and causes me to analyze other aspects of my life. There really is no reason why I can't achieve whatever I set my mind to. I am no longer my own limitation.

Eventually I start to drift away from the match sprints. I become bored racing the same people week in and week out. The field is shrinking and the competition dropping. The passion is waning. I have already established a solid foundation of victories. The losses give me more education on my weaknesses, which I can use for improvement. What I find more enjoyable are time trials, which are considered the race of truth. My opponent is the man in the mirror. He is my toughest opponent, always pushing for another PR. I am my own worst critic. No one will ever be as hard on me as I am. This is a trait that comes from my childhood abuse. This type of competition forces me to find peace within myself.

As I begin my journey into time trialing, I find great peace in the solitude of the event. Whether it be the track or the road, it's just me, the bike, the clock, and whatever demons rattle around in my head. No room for self-doubt or low self-esteem. The longer the time trial, the harder it is mentally to push through the physical pain and the desire to stop. Quitting is never an option. The sense of satisfaction and accomplishment when I am done is huge. Whether I set a new PR or simply put in a solid performance, knowing that I left it all on the bike is deeply gratifying.

2017 is my comeback year on the bike. I train hard and claw my way back to optimal race form through hard work, focus, discipline, and tenacity—the same tenacity that brought me through the fire storm of my abusive childhood, the decades of internal torment from the sexual abuse, and my personal lifelong battle with addiction.

Throughout the countless dark days that follow my crash, and the roller coaster of emotions, I hold out hope that I will have the honor of competing at the UCI World's Masters Track Cycling Championships and representing the United States on the World's stage. I had set my sights on that goal ever since the venue was announced in late 2015, a few months before my crash. The World's Championships had not been held on U.S. soil for over a decade. In 2017 it would be held in Los Angeles, California. This could be a once in a lifetime opportunity. I know immediately I want to compete. I *need* to compete. Not many people get that chance. I have to take my shot. I also know that I will not go if I am not ready. I do not want to be an embarrassment to myself, my country, and my family.

As I ramp up into the 2017 season, I still have a lot of inner beasts to face down. The disappointment and frustration of the senseless crash, the fact that I have been blameless in the series of unfortunate events, and my lack of control over what happened leave me questioning if I should be racing at all in *any* discipline, much less track racing. But I know I still have unfinished business with the sport. I take each day as it is given—making the most of the opportunities, accepting the mediocrity or setbacks, and relishing the forward progress.

As the season progresses, I can tell I am getting stronger both physically and mentally. Because of my improvement, I am more confident in everything I attempt. I am blessed to be surrounded by good people who encourage and support me. Their advice always seems timely and priceless. To prepare for the possibility of World's, I have set a short-term goal for myself: If I can do well at the regional competition—which take place two months before the big event—then I will go to Worlds.

Regionals arrive and I feel calm. No jitters. I know why I am here...I am racing the man in the mirror. As a match sprinter, I will need to qualify fast enough to make the finals. Only the top eight make it. Match Sprints are seeded by the flying 200-meter time trial (200TT). The fastest eight riders in the field are seeded for a one-on-one Match Sprint for the finals. It's an elimination process. The slowest qualifier races the fastest qualifier in round one. That winner moves up the ladder and that loser moves down to the fifth through eighth finals. You can have a slow qualifier but win the Match Sprint and still move up the ladder to finals. I've never had a great 200TT time, but I have managed to beat some of the fastest qualifiers in Match Sprints. My PR of 12.8 was good enough for eighth place in the 200TT. That meant that I would be racing the fastest rider in the first round. My competitor had qualified nearly a second faster than me. It is a game of nerves for the first lap and a half. Then he attacked and razored to the line. I lost by a wheel. Clearly a defeat on paper, but still a victory for me. My competitor is a multi-World champion who holds over thirty World records.

With my confidence boosted, I move onto the fifth through eighth elimination round. This is a "four-up," which is much more difficult to control. A standard match sprint race only has two riders. For the elimination round there are four riders. With three other riders to keep an eye on and three other riders keeping an eye on me, the opportunities to attack are minimized. The match sprint is only a two-lap race, so the energy builds to a peak in a very short time. The tension, speed, and jockeying for position are building throughout lap one. As we enter lap two, one rider begins to razor, increasing from a slow roll to a full-on sprint. This forces everyone else in the race to follow suit or get left far behind. Another rider attacks and rider three follows. I am last in line but luckily for me I have an explosive jump. I attack with a fury that sends me flying past the first three riders and slingshot into the lead by three bike lengths. I am able to hold off their counterattacks to the line and win by a bike length. I finish fifth overall.

With that display of tactical racing and explosive speed I know I am ready for World's. Sign me up!

SPOKES

"Aggregate marginal gains" is a term I learned while training during this time. It is a method used by pro athletes who compete at the highest level of their chosen craft. The theory behind it is that as you become more skilled, the improvements or "gains" become less frequent and lower in volume. For example, as a match sprinter, when I first started racing, I could expect to improve my 200TT time by half a second or three tenths of a second. As I became faster, I would hit a plateau.   When I did improve after that, the gains were marginal—say, only one tenth of a second. The pro riders have much more sophisticated equipment and can measure their improvements down to the hundredth of a second. These improvements are known as "Aggregate Marginal Gains."

This concept is the same in bike racing as it is in life. The longer we spend mastering our task, the more incremental the gains…but they definitely add up and each one matters.

CHAPTER THIRTEEN
WORLD'S CHAMPIONSHIP 2017

Your next level of success may not come from what you are focusing on. Sometimes it comes from an unrelated source or someplace unexpected. Other times a failure may lead to a lesson, which leads to another level.

Walking into the VELO Sports Centre in Carson just south of Los Angeles is always a special experience. It is a world class facility. With a seating capacity of only 2,700, it has an intimate feel. However, the relatively small crowd also adds to the emphasis of the track. The smooth-as-glass polished Siberian pine track dominates the atmosphere and the countless flags from every country in the world put an exclamation mark on it. When you step into the velodrome you know you are stepping onto hallowed ground. This is a mecca with a lifetime of history. These walls have witnessed the agony of defeat and the sweet splendor of victory.

The day before the race we have open track practice. That means that everyone is doing something different in terms of their efforts, and the various languages spoken do not provide a common conduit for communication. Welcome to the chaos! Little do I know before arriving that every single pen on the infield is already marked and claimed by someone. That leaves me hanging out in the aisle with nowhere to sit other than the floor. Less than an ideal situation but I improvise. Out come my bike rollers (used for indoor training), which become my makeshift chair. Problem solved. I gear up, look for an opening on the track, and start my warmup.

The VELO Sports Centre is an Olympic-size track built for the 1984 games. The total distance around the oval track is 250 meters. The front and back straight have fifteen-degree banking. The corners each have a forty-five-degree banking and are two stories tall. The outer edge of the track is encompassed by a metal railing much like the banister on a flight of stairs. The inner edge of the track is flat with a wire mesh fence surrounding the infield. When riding up on the rail—which is the longest way around the track—the minimum speed required to prevent gravity from sending you crashing down—is twenty miles per hour. The benefit of riding up on the rail is that you can build up a lot of speed coming down the steep bank into the sprinter's lane, which is the shortest way around the track. There are only about a dozen people on the track, so it is relatively easy to monitor who is where and what they are doing. I roll around up on the rail and that's when it hits me. I am about to race at the World's Championships! Tomorrow is my big day. My heart rate spikes. My breathing becomes short, and my chest is tight. OK, time to go back to the infield, meditate, and start over. I need this practice session to be smooth and set the tone for tomorrow's race.

I am no stranger to starting over. I have reset countless times in my life with addiction and overcoming my childhood trauma. I have learned to reset almost by second nature. My study of Buddhism has taught me to be present in the moment. Years of racing have taught me to control what I can control. I have countless tactics to employ in any given situation. That is the beautiful thing about life; each day before has taught me a lesson to prepare me for this day.

Once on the infield I find a quiet corner, which is not an easy task, and start my Qi Gong meditation. I have no idea what the other riders think when they see me standing there with my eyes closed bouncing softly on my heels and my body vibrating from head to toe. I really don't care. I am finding peace in my space. As I feel the serenity wash over my body and my energy begin to center, my rapid breathing finds the calming rhythm. A few more minutes of visualization of my 200TT effort and I am ready to get back on the track with a calmness in my body and mind.

The second attempt at a warmup is much smoother. No jitters, just another warmup. The track is busy now with approximately twenty riders. The thing to remember about track racing is that you have to be aware of your surroundings at all times. Generally, the riders tend to all bunch up even if they are doing different efforts. That provides gaps in space where you can move freely and safely. I spend the next twenty minutes reading the field, making short efforts, and feeling the rhythm of the track. Once I am confident that I have found my fast line, I return to the infield to change into my race gear. The bikes used to race on the velodrome are fixed gear. That is, they are direct drive with no brakes. I use a smaller gear that is easy to ride to warm up. Once my body and mind are ready, I switch to a higher gear for racing. Although I am not in competition on this day, it is still important to use the same gear as I will use for the race the next day to get a feel for it and make sure the bike is working properly.

Once I have recovered from the huge cardio effort and switched to my race gear, I am ready to resume practice on the track. The track is still busy with riders from every corner of the globe. It is exhilarating to be a part of it. I quickly find a smooth rhythm on the rail, rolling fast down the banking into the stretch and floating across the top of the turns…maximizing the energy created while minimizing the effort expended. What once felt uncomfortable and tightened my chest now feels natural.

With a good amount of speed, I approach the marker signaling my jump up out of the saddle. I follow the curve of the corner as it descends into turn four and propels me onto the front stretch. It feels like I am literally getting launched like a rocket. All I can do is hang on and pilot this thing between my legs into turn one, where the G-forces attempt to push me up track into a much slower line. The fastest way around the track is at the bottom closest to the infield. I am pushing down on the left handlebar and relaxing the upper body so that I flow with the energy instead of fighting it. Much as in life, I am finding the rhythm and flowing with the energy.

I change the energy when it begins to work against me by altering the input. Relax, flow, rhythm. Pure Zen follows. I tuck as low as possible into the drops and become one with the bike through turn two onto the backstretch, keeping the cadence up. I am sticking to the black line as it is the shortest route around the track. I tuck tight into the corners of turns three and four. Hitting the front stretch always feels like hitting a wall. My legs are screaming to stop. My lungs are screaming for more air. My body is spent. My peripheral vision begins to narrow as my oxygen-deprived brain tries to process everything that is happening. I push down hard on the pedals on the front stretch for the last bit of effort I can squeeze from my exhausted body.

I go back to the infield for a full recovery before one more effort. Everything is complete in preparation for tomorrow's World's Championship competition. I need to make sure I have fresh legs. My mind is calm; my body is strong.

I spend the rest of the day visiting Muscle Beach with my family. It is good to revisit the place where my childhood friend, mentor, and nephew Joe began his power lifting career. Times have changed a lot since then, but it still feels good to drift back in time and feel grounded in the memories of laughter we shared. I need to keep busy so that my mind doesn't wander to the dark place of self-doubt and create unnecessary anxiety.

I wake the morning of the World's Championships with a calm sense of readiness. I know that I have done all that I can do to prepare for this day. There is nothing left but to deliver the best effort possible. Leave nothing in the tank. Focus on the details. Absorb the moment. Breathe. Relax. Enjoy.

Breakfast with my family is filled with lively conversation. I make one last gear check before Marsha drives me to the hotel where Diallo, my longtime teammate and training partner, is staying. Diallo and I have a decade-long history of pushing each other to new and higher levels of performance. *Iron sharpens iron.* I find comfort in his smile and the familiarity of his face. Two of the officials from my home track are there officiating at World's. More familiar faces! This makes me smile and adds another comfort level. Chatter fills the car as we are chauffeured to the track by Marsha. This day definitely feels special.

Once at the track I take the lead by telling everyone where to put things and it all goes very smoothly. Everyone seems to be there to help me succeed. My emotions are all over the place. My nerves go from calm to red-line and my heart rate follows. I know that if I am to find any peace in this day, I will need to get a grip on those emotions. So I meditate. Right there on the infield, I close my eyes, block out the world around me, and do my Qi Gong. I am totally at peace with myself and my surroundings. The effects don't last long, so I do it again. Diallo is there to help with whatever I need, but this is something I must do alone. It is important for me to prep my equipment and make sure all my gear is in its place. It's a ritual honed with time and repetition.

At the appointed time, the racing begins. It seems odd to me There is no opening ceremony, no welcome announcement, just a brief announcement to commence racing. Now I have to figure out what time I will be on the track. I try to time the riders ahead of me and calculate when I will be racing. I don't feel like I have a very good grip on the time frame. I am staring at the start list for my event trying to figure it out when a familiar voice says, "What heat are you in?" I turn to see former World's Champion and elite pro Joanne Kiesenowski from New Zealand. What a welcome face! I tell her Heat 10 and she replies, "Oh, you will be racing at 3:30 to 3:45." Shocked, I thank her and wonder how she can calculate that so quickly. I make a mental note of the time and thank her again. She must have sensed that I was nervous because she starts talking to me and asks me random questions to ease my mind. I had only seen Joanne for the first time the day before and here she is now, giving me last minute coaching advice. How lucky am I?

Now preparing for my time in the race, I make my way back to my bike and do another gear check. The start list is posted at the opposite end of the track from where I had set up. It's only a 250-meter track but it takes a while to thread my way through all the riders. I am working hard to manage my sensory overload. Since the concussion from my 2016 crash, I have had tremendous bouts of sensory overload when in public. Over time I learned to manage it by minimizing facial recognition. I trained myself to watch the shoes. I could tell by the walk which direction the oncoming person was going to turn and didn't have to look at their face to figure it out. When you see a person's face your brain automatically does a scan to see if you know that person. By the time we are in our forties we have over 40,000 faces in memory. It doesn't take long to get exhausted when you've had as many head injuries as I have had. Then the nausea sets in. The only way to turn the tide is to leave the environment for a quiet place to meditate.

I don't need to do another gear check, but it makes me feel better and gives me something to focus on besides my upcoming qualifier round. I get on the rollers but feel unsure how much to warm up. I don't want to ramp up too early and peak before qualifying. I also don't want to be caught out cold and have dead legs. There are so many details to sort out for my first World's Championships. The nerves and the voices in my head threaten to send me into a dark downward spiral. My time is getting closer. I am getting nervous, so I go to the bike check even though it is too early. I have to know that it will pass inspection before it is go time. I hand her over and watched tentatively until all specs are certified. With thirty minutes still to kill before I am on track, I fidget with my bike on the rollers and try to remain calm. Under the circumstances, I am doing pretty well.

With fifteen minutes to go, I make my way over to the start line. Bike check one more time. Now to sit and wait. Joanne shows up at that moment and starts asking if I am ready. Did I bike check? What is my heat number? Telling me to relax. She really did help. I might have been a hot mess if she had not shown up at key moments to bring calm to my world.

Then it was time. Zack, a local official says, "Mike you're up." It seems so calm the way the words roll off his tongue. I go to the rail and take up a spot with five other riders ahead of me. One by one the referee waves them on track. I am up next. Diallo asks me how I feel. I tell him, "Hungry." Not in the sense of needing food but in the sense of I am ready to compete at the highest level of my career. I am hungry to give my best performance. To leave it all on the track. To empty the tank.

I say a prayer, cross my heart, and point to the heavens, telling Joe, "This one's for you, brother." The referee points at me. "Are you ready?" I nod my head and say yes. He steps aside and I get a big push. I am racing at the World's Championships!

The velodrome falls silent in my ears, although I know it hasn't. I am so focused I don't even notice anyone in the stands. It is just me and the bike on the track. I start my windup. With two laps to go I feel like I have gone out too fast. I am really tight. My cardio is already screaming. I stay focused on my windup and try to relax my breathing by taking a few deep breaths. It doesn't really seem to calm me. With one and a half laps to go I start to push the pace.

Coming through turn three into four I see my green line marking the start of my jump. With intense focus I get up out of the saddle and stomp on the pedals with all the strength available in my legs, pulling up on the opposite handlebar like I am trying to twist the bike in half. I roll through turn four and onto the front stretch, driving the pedals hard underneath me. The bell rings, sounding the final lap. I drive hard into turn one, slamming the bike under me and diving down into the sprinter's lane. The G-forces want to push me up track. I push down hard on the left handlebar and lean the bike to be perpendicular with the forty-five-degree banked corner. Riding almost horizontally takes some practice, as it is counterintuitive to how you learn to ride a bike in its normal upright position.

The back stretch seems to come at me from nowhere. I put my head down and push hard on the pedals, trying to squeeze another ten watts from my exhausted legs. Rolling into turn three I can feel the legs suffering a bit. I focus on the black line and dig deeper to keep my cadence up. Coming through turn four I am fading fast. I have no lungs and my limbs feel like noodles. I still have to push down the front stretch and cross the line for my time. The line seems to approach at the speed of a snail. It is as if time is slowing as I ride down the front stretch.

With the last bit of energy I can muster, I throw the bike across the line for the finish. 13.7 seconds. The slowest time I have posted all season. I have consistently posted low 12's on my home track. The only similarity is that I ride the same bike on both tracks. I was crushed. By my standards my time was pathetic. I had not posted anything in the 13's since my rookie year.

I would later realize that by World's competition standards my time was not pathetic at all, but still not good enough to qualify in the top eight riders who move on to finals. There is no doubt that I am disappointed. But I have also just competed at World level. It doesn't get any bigger than this for me. There is no chance for another level…only faster times.

I am overwhelmed with emotion. I have worked so hard and overcome so much to have a place on the World's stage. Seventeen months earlier I didn't know if I would ever ride again much less race. The road to recovery from the 2016 crash was littered with more setbacks—or *resets*, as I renamed them—even beyond the healing itself. Just as I was nearly healed, a car accident had set me back, followed by two more over the next four months for a total of three in six months! None of them were my fault. I was stopped in traffic and rear ended each time. Each crash left me with another concussion which reminded me how fragile my brain was. While the subsequent head injuries were insignificant in comparison to the one from the 2016 crash (which rendered me unconscious), they all add up. I had to go beyond. Once again, the tenacity I learned as a child while overcoming the abuse had given me the tools to persevere once again through all these setbacks.

Competing at World's teaches me many things. Some are expected and somewhat obvious, like the boost in self-confidence. Others are unexpected, like coming in at the slowest time of the season despite all my training and preparation. As I analyze every detail, from the gear choice to my fitness level to the windup to the line into the corners and countless others, I come to realize that it really doesn't matter. What is truly important is that I gave everything I had to perform my best on that day. And I know that when I face the man in the mirror, I can hold my head high knowing that I gave it all for that ride and held nothing back. Sure, there are things I can do differently now that I know more. But hindsight is always clearer than forecasting the future.

At the Word's event I learn one extremely valuable lesson about racing: Just because a particular line *feels* fast does not mean that it *is* fast. I didn't have the ability to time my efforts on the VELO track prior to the competition. That is the disadvantage of training alone. That knowledge would have made a difference in my time. It would most likely not have been significant enough to place in the finals, but at least it would have been faster. Emphasis on lesson learned; what gets measured gets improved.

Make no mistake, I went to World's to bring my best. I had no illusions of a podium finish or even making the finals. The top eight riders are all retired professionals who have forgotten more about racing than I will ever know. I wanted to compete to prove that I had the self-confidence to do it. There are a lot of people much faster than me. I spoke with some of them leading up to the event. They lacked the confidence to compete.

On October 10, 2017, I rank 32nd in the world in the Flying 200TT. There are thirty-four riders in this field. In my opinion, 32nd isn't anything to brag about. But I showed up! All the others who could have beat me but didn't show up...they don't get to tell their grandkids how they competed at World's Championships! I beat everyone else who didn't show up. If you want to increase your chances of success at anything, the first and most important step is to SHOW UP!

I also learn something that really surprises me, something I never expected to come out of this competition. Upon my return home there is an outpouring of support from my friends, family, and followers on social media. Many people say, "Congratulations!" and "I'm proud of what you've accomplished!" Then they follow with "You inspired me to do _________." Fill in the blank. Everything from a simple goal of getting into the gym twice a week, to training for a triathlon or half marathon, to simply riding a long distance. People used my experience as their inspiration. Unbelievable! And that is truly the most rewarding aspect of this competition. I was able to inspire others. That is a beautiful thing.

I take a month off from training after competing at World's. I need a break from the regimen. After three weeks, I become restless and bored. I am losing focus. There are a couple of things I really enjoy about not training, like being able to eat guilt free. Anything and everything is on the menu and I don't have to think about how it will impact my performance or if I will gain that extra pound. The other thing is not shaving my arms and legs. I don't have to maintain those guns! One less project. Relaxation at its best!

In spite of the perks, it is fulfilling to get back to training. It is much less intense than the routine leading up to World's, but still rewarding. I now have focus. I regain the drive and enjoy the discipline. It becomes clear that training is a necessary part of my addiction recovery. Without that focus it would be easier for me to drift back the old ways and make poor choices. I cannot simply train day in and day out without goals or measurements of success because I will get burned out and lose direction. There is a fine line and beautiful balance with training, competing, rest, and inner peace.

Although I am no longer formally racing in any capacity, the competition with myself is still there, even with something as routine as riding my bike to work. I'm commuting; it's just going from point A to point B. That's the goal, which seems simple. But it's not for me. I need to do it as fast as I can, as hard as I can. What is my sustained effort for today? How much effort am I going to put in? What wattage am I putting out? What's my heart rate? I need to know all these things. The first thing I do when I get to my destination is pull out my phone and track it all. Then I can compare this ride today with my PR and where I am at. Is my fitness going up or down, or am I holding my own? I am relentless. It's almost like, "Fuck, Mike…can't you just have a fun ride without chasing numbers?" But this IS my fun.

And so with this lesson another level of success is achieved. It is just another affirmation that I am doing the right things. It is the catalyst for my continued improvement and success. There is always another level.

SPOKES

Change can be the most powerful or the most destructive thing a person can do. For the wandering adolescent on the right path who makes a change of friends and ends up being influenced to try drinking and drugs, that change is the first step down the long road of addiction and recovery. For the addict who puts down their vice for the last time, change is powerful.

When change is good, it brings a new burst of energy. The mind is alive with renewed hope and ideas. The body follows the invigorating sensation, and everything seems possible. The problem for most people is that change seems scary, and the uncertainty paralyzes their ability to move forward. The comfort of the moment can lock you down. Even for addicts facing a life of despair the thought of change and a better life can seem unattainable. I always thought I could change my drinking habits. I told myself for decades "I am in control. I can stop at two drinks." I was wrong. I was kidding myself. Now that I have taken the steps to change from within, I am energized and empowered in every aspect of my life! There are no limits, no boundaries for my success. There is always another level. I do not know what that level is, but I know that when I am mentally, physically, and spiritually ready for it, the opportunity will present itself and once again it will be time for a change.

CHAPTER FOURTEEN
FINDING PEACE

Over time, the positive change will be evident not only to you…but to everyone around you.

As I continue to be sober, more clarity creeps into my thought process. As a recovering addict I look back at all the times I indulged to extreme excess. I noticed a recurring pattern that I had never observed before. After a binge that seemed like it should have killed me, I felt a sense of immortality. Somehow, I felt as if I had beat the odds. It was empowering and beckoned me to do it again. There were countless times when I would think "This is clean vodka. I know I can drink half a fifth and still walk the straight line tomorrow." And I did. There were other times when I faked my way through the day. Now that I have been sober for years, I recognize that false sense of power. I now know that it was quite the opposite. I was the prisoner to the addiction, not the other way around. I was powerless. Now that I am free from the chains, I am the most powerful man in the room.

The brief sense of euphoria I experienced in the sliver of time between the first drink and the first drink too many has been replaced with daily happiness. I have found peace in my relationship with myself. I find peace in a bike ride even when the weather isn't perfect. Sometimes it is the sunrise. The pure joy of spending time with the people I care about brings me a level of happiness that I was chasing for decades in the bottom of a bottle. I could never find it then, and I am grateful I have found it now. I cannot change the past; I can only change how I react to it. I choose to break the cycle of violence and abuse every day. I choose to let go of the hate and lead a peaceful life. I choose a better path.

Not every day is sunshine and rainbows. There are still dark moments when I fight depression. There are still times when the rage boils up inside of me and the hate comes rushing out like a dam unleashed. I have learned to acknowledge those feelings and confront them, so they become powerless over me. *Control what I can control.* I cannot control the emotion that overwhelms me; I am human. But I can control how I react to it. I became an addict "a little at a time and then all at once." I am staying sober the same way. So many things in life happen that way. *A little at a time, and then all at once.*

Sometimes I am asked by someone "Why are you not angry?" They are referring to my childhood and all the ugly things that I endured. I used to be angry. I was filled with hatred for the old man. It faded over time as I healed and let go of the shame and guilt for those things I had no control over. As I grew up, I watched both my parents wake up every morning bitter at the entire world. Bitter that they had to face another day on earth. I swore I would not be like that. I have strived to be everything they were not. I want to be the best version of me despite all I have endured.

The truth is, I do still have anger. I still have rage in me. I deal with it by letting it go each day, each time I wake up. I release it through physical exertion. When I hit the weights, I give it everything I have. Sometimes I lift until I collapse. The release of anger is uplifting. I have internally conquered those who put me down in my past. I am physically and mentally stronger. When I am on the bike—whether it be the trainer, the spin bike, a training ride, or cruising with my grandson—it doesn't matter. When I give maximum effort in a sprint or a climb and turn myself inside out, I am letting go of that anger and hatred. There is no space in my life for the past or for rage. When I let go of the anger it can no longer control me. The people that did those things to me can no longer control me. I move forward.

Let it go. Whatever it is, let it go. Move past it. You have two choices that will lead to success: move past it or move on. If you move past it, you heal and so do the people around you. If you move on you put it behind and heal along with the people around you. Regardless of what it is—death, lost love, regret, poor choices—let it go. Do not dwell on it. This doesn't mean you bury it and forget about it. Quite the opposite; you acknowledge it, and you deal with it. You deal with the emotion, the frustration, the pain. Do not let the past consume you. *Our history defines who we are, but our choices define who we become.*

One thing I would like to make clear: I achieved sobriety and peace through a lot of hard work. I'm proud to say I did it without rehab; I've never been to an Alcoholics Anonymous meeting. I have nothing against these programs. They are powerful tools and I know many people who have found great benefit with them. They just weren't for me. I encourage anyone going through the battle of addiction to consider rehab or AA or any other support group that brings you closer to sobriety and freedom. They do a lot of great things. Do what's right for you.

I'm proud of the fact that I faced my demons and beat my addiction and changed the course of my path working hard and tirelessly given the tools at my disposal. And when I didn't have the tools that I needed to succeed, I sought out a solution with utter determination. Nobody is going to just give you sobriety or peace or closure. You have to work your ass off to get it and hold it! *It never gets easy; you just get stronger.*

People wonder how I can talk about all of this…my past, the abuse, the addiction. It wasn't always easy. But I have worked through it and accepted that I can't change anything, and I can't get revenge. The shame fades the more I share my story with people who have been through something similar. Talking about the abuse is the easy part. The hard part is thinking about other people close to me who have their own stories and their own trauma, and they haven't yet worked through them.

It took a lifetime, but I finally figured it out. There is a direct correlation between sharing and inner peace. To give—whether it be something physical like a meal or a coffee, or mental/spiritual like knowledge or empathy—brings me a great sense of fulfillment. Maybe it's standing in line at a Starbucks, and I buy the person behind me a coffee. Most of the time people don't know what to do with this random act of kindness. They stutter and fumble and politely decline. I insist and you can see the warm glow of happiness move across their face. It's a simple coffee, but it's as if they were given a bonus.

It's the same when I share about my experience with abuse. There are times when people come into my life through various channels. As the relationship grows, it becomes obvious that some of them need support. When we first meet, they have no idea what I have been through, but the forces of the universe have brought us together. People tend to share a lot of personal information with me—life stuff they cannot tell anyone else. It is not uncommon for someone I know at a social level, or maybe just a casual acquaintance, to share deep personal stories. These people do not fall under the category of "friends." Yet they will confide in me with some very private details. They never ask for advice about their situation, and I don't offer any. They seem to only need to let it go. You can see the relief on their face when they have spoken their truth. They know their situation is safe with me. The amount of trust I am given is humbling. It's as if I am helping others by feeling their pain.

There is an unspoken connection amongst survivors of sexual abuse. They recognize the pain of others who have gone through similar experiences and survived. It's not constant. It's not like we all instantly know each other. But there is something about the mannerisms that provide clues. It's almost like a secret society. We rarely talk about our pain and recovery openly because that exposes our shame. When I connect with a survivor, words are not immediately spoken. There is a look in their eyes. A look of sorrow. My role is to listen, to empathize, and to offer some wisdom. Whatever the situation is, I know that to continue the path of success, I must give when I can.

I have had countless people tell me that I should be a life coach. I can't even comprehend that. I never really felt like I had anything to offer. I always thought someone who is a life coach should be flawless. As I healed the emotional scars and beat the addiction, I realized that this is not at all true. In fact, perhaps some of the best life coaches around are people who have been knocked down and got back up. People who have risen from the ashes. I realize now that I can offer advice, solace, and empathy for anyone who needs it.

Sometimes all that is needed to start healing is to let go.

SPOKES

To be alive or truly live? This is a question I have pondered for many hours. It is easy to go through life on autopilot. Working diligently, providing for your family, paying the bills. A life of simple mediocrity. We breathe in, we breathe out; our heart beats; our brain processes information. These are the things that define us as being "alive." But what about the life we "live?" To truly live we must seek a fulfilling life for ourselves. For me that has come to mean giving to others and forgiving myself. There is great joy in helping others achieve what they thought they could not. There is great joy in seeing someone's face light up with their achievement. I have been blessed with teaching countless kids to ride a bike. The look of pure joy on their face as they experience freedom for the first time is priceless. The look of relief on their parents faces as they witness this great accomplishment of their child is very rewarding. It is truly a beautiful thing.

The tenacity that propels me forward every day (sometimes in the face of adversity) was learned when I was a child. Back then it was a survival mechanism. Today it is a gift. Little did my parents know, as they dispensed the daily abuse, that I would turn that negative into a positive. I can be beaten and broken but never defeated. Today I stand tall and proud not as a victim or survivor but as a success. In everything that really matters in life—my marriage, my children, my career, my life— I have beaten the odds. For this I am grateful.

CHAPTER FIFTEEN
THE OUTER DEMONS

Experiences like this leave a scar on the soul. Time takes the edge off, but the scars are still there for anyone who dares to look. Scars remind us that the past is real. They also shape us for our future challenges.

I had been sober for about four years when I came to the realization that I needed to deal with something I had been avoiding for decades. I had faced my inner demons back in 2015 when I got sober and started therapy. But now I had to confront the outer demons. I had to stare down the history I had with my parents.

As the decades passed after my father's death, through my years working in the Midwest and then moving to the West Coast, I remained distant from my mother. After I left Michigan, I think it became obvious that I was my own man. Nobody was going to keep me down. Mary no longer had control over me. On the rare occasions when we did meet, she showered me with praise and gifts. She always insisted on paying for lunch or dinner or coffee even though she was living on a fixed income. Mary would always buy the kids anything they wanted and sometimes even things they really didn't want. It seemed her way of trying to make amends for the past choices with me. She was stubborn as the day is long and arguing with her was a waste of time, not to mention it always created a scene.

After I moved to Seattle and built a very lucrative career, she would praise me and tell everyone how successful I was. None of this changed what had happened in the past. The abuse was a stark reality. There was never an apology or even a hint of remorse. I never asked those things. I knew it wouldn't change anything. I just woke up every day stronger than the day before. No apology would erase or justify the abuse from my parents. Powers beyond my control put me in that situation. I not only survived but I persevered.

Mary passed away in 2009 and I continued to have little communication with my sister or extended family. It's not that we didn't get along; I just really had nothing to say. I had a feeling of estrangement but never took the time to analyze it and understand why.

My sister is fifteen years older than me. I was not planned. I grew up being referred to as "the accident." That's what my parents always told me. Whenever my mother said it, she followed the remark with a laugh. I never knew what that meant other than I got the feeling it wasn't a good thing. She always told me that the old man was in great shape until I was born and that's when he gained weight. What I heard was "You are an accident and it's your fault your father is fat." If someone else had said these words, they would be construed as a joke. But I am sure my mother believed and meant them. I was the excuse for his bad eating habits and lack of exercise. After all, someone had to be his scapegoat. He would never take responsibility for that himself. It might as well be an innocent child. This is just one of the reasons I have battled low self-esteem throughout my life.

For most of my adult life, I had kept a distance from my sister. There was a lot of history in our relationship from my younger years, and those memories were not very pleasant for me. I had been a young man filled with anger and inner conflict while constantly living with my growing addiction. I perceived that no matter what the topic, my sister always sided with our mother. As Mary became elderly and in need of constant care, my sister provided that. I had walked away decades before. Yet, despite my anger, I had a lot of guilt about not being supportive as they went through the many health challenges that aging brings about. I felt ashamed because it seemed like that's what children are supposed to do. They were supposed to care for an elderly parent. Everyone else was doing it.

Eventually I realized that my situation was unique because of the childhood abuse. As I healed, I also came to realize that my lack of trust for my sister was unfounded. She had no knowledge of what I went through until long after Mary passed. It took a lot of healing, acceptance, and forgiveness for us to develop the relationship we had lost. It was well worth it!

As we grew closer, I realized our parents were broken well before I came along. I am not sure what event or chain of events caused their pain. What I do know is that there is a long lineage of good people who made me who I am today. I will not allow two people to erase the foundation of who I am. I broke the cycle of violence and abuse, and that is powerful.

My relationship with my sister really changed when she came to Seattle to visit after my crash in 2016. For the first time, we talked. I mean we *really* communicated. It was the first time in my life that I can remember us interacting like adult siblings. It was a very empowering experience. I finally understood that during all those decades my anger towards my mother had been directed at my sister for giving compassion to the person who failed to show me any as a child. I now understood why the relationship with my sister had suffered, and with that knowledge came the power to change. It was such a gift! I was blessed with a sister I had never really known.

I always tell her that she is so much stronger than me. She stuck by Mary's side to the very end. I left. I never looked back, I just walked away. My sister disagrees. She said it took more courage to leave than to stay. Neither path was an easy road. Sometimes life does not give you good choices…only options. Now we text almost daily and talk on the phone weekly. But most importantly, we laugh. Deep belly laughs that only siblings can share.

The closeness I felt with my sister was comforting, but there was still a door left opened. I had worked on my inner demons, but I needed closure with the outer ones. As helpful as the therapy and other tools had been, I needed a more tangible showdown. I knew from the depths of my soul that the next step was to return to the house where I grew up. I was scared at first…intimidated and living in denial. As I continued to process the thought of going back, it became more important for me to face my parents (both long dead) and tell them how I felt. I knew it would be difficult and emotional, but I also knew that I could work through the fear and face them. My father had been in the ground for decades and by this time my mother had been gone for over ten years, so there was no one alive whom I could confront and say, "FUCK YOU!" There was no one to receive my anger. So, I did the next best thing. I flew back to Michigan and visited the place where I had grown up. My sister went with me.

Very few people ever got a glimpse of the truth behind the walls of the big brick house where I was raised. Everyone looked up to the old man as a pillar of the community. They thought my mother was a "sweet old lady." People unrelated to her called her "Grandma Mary." The old man got away with it. He died an early death. Sometimes I wonder what

I would say to him if we could meet. What would I ask? I have no words. There is no point in asking "why?" Whatever justification he could make in his own twisted mind would be pathetically inept for me. The same goes for my mother.

My sister and I drove out to the old homestead one day in her truck. We parked on the road and walked around the property. The house had long been sold to strangers and it had changed a lot from when I was a kid. But it was still there.

I had written a letter before the trip which I read as I stood at the end of the steep driveway where I had spent countless hours riding my bike as a child. It was fulfilling to see the broken shell of a once pristine estate. There was an unspoken justice to bear witness to the shambles. How fitting, I thought, that this once stately property was now akin to a forgotten junkyard.

I took in all the scenery as I read the letter to my parents with a trembling voice and breathed a sigh of relief through tear-filled eyes. In short, the letter said *You fucked up! You both were horrible parents. I broke the cycle. Fuck you! I won!* I felt the heavy weight of my past leave my body. I crumpled the letter in my fist and threw it on the ground and walked away. I hugged my sister, thankful for her presence as I faced this demon. We held hands and skipped away finally feeling free like a couple of kids. I never looked back. It was liberating!

I had rented a bike from a local shop, which we had brought out in the back of my sister's truck. After reading the letter I rode the three and a half miles to my old school like I had done so many times back then. It was a ride I had made over and over during the one good year of my childhood after the sexual abuse stopped and before the addiction began. It was just one sliver of time in my youth. I let go of a lot of pain on that ride. There was a rage inside me that was finally released. The hills felt much smaller and the distance much shorter than I remembered. I pedaled hard and I rode the past off my wheel. I turned myself inside out and it felt invigorating. When it was done, my sister picked me up at the Methodist church across from my old school and we left.

Building up the courage to go back to the place where I experienced so much pain was the hardest thing I have ever had to do in my adult life. It was a very emotionally draining task. I had anticipated a lot of pain, and I was right. Although I felt better, I still didn't feel entirely free. I had hoped I would feel a great sense of satisfaction…a sense of peace. Some type of immediate healing and relief. I did not. I was left with the same gaping hole that I had tried to fill with alcohol. I was disappointed and became filled with despair. I really thought this would be the one thing that would heal me completely. What I didn't understand is that healing is subject to all other progress in life. It amounts to aggregate marginal gains. Think of one aggregate marginal gain as the thickness of a sheet of paper. One sheet is almost nothing. But if you keep stacking until you have ten or twenty sheets, now you have some measure of gains over time. Keep stacking until you have fifty sheets and now you have significant, noticeable improvement. They all add up and each one matters. I learned this with racing and with physical training. I was foolish to think it would be any different with healing from my past.

At some point I realized that I needed to let go of the hate I had for my father. This is something I am still working on. For decades I dealt with the pain of my childhood and hatred for my parents by not dealing with it. That doesn't just go away with one trip. I thought I could put it all in the rear-view mirror and it would fade away. What I didn't know is that everything I wasn't dealing with was accumulating on the rear bumper. My way of coping was to move away from where I grew up and sever all relationships with anyone associated with my parents. In hindsight that was a bad decision. It not only hurt a lot of people who cared about me, but it also prevented a relationship between my children and their aunts, uncles, and cousins.

There will always be a void where I walked away but at least now I am moving forward. As time passed and I got back into my daily rhythm, the healing started to sink in. I am glad I did the hard work to return to my past and face those demons. I have come to an understanding that it was a necessary step in the long journey. It was hard work, and it was worth it. I spent a lot of decades hiding from my past. That didn't work. I spent another decade dancing with the wicked mistress of addiction, always one drink away from disaster and constantly trying to convince myself I wasn't an alcoholic. That didn't work either. Once I gathered up the courage to face my demons, I was finally able to heal permanently.

There is a sense of knowing and calmness that has come to me since revisiting my childhood home. It was very empowering to write the letter I read at the foot of my old driveway. It brought me to another level of healing. This healing was more like a fire burning out. It left slowly. It left scars as a reminder of the past, but I now have a new foundation to build from. This foundation is peace...which comes from forgiveness.

SPOKES

Letter To My Parents, Delivered May 1, 2018

Ray and Mary: I will not call you by parental names of Dad and Mom. You never earned that right to carry that title.

Ray: You ruled your world with an iron fist. Your extreme outbursts of brutal physical abuse were unwarranted under any circumstances. Your repeated sexual abuse…cannot be justified under any circumstances. Ever. There is no excuse or reason to justify those actions carried out over decades.

Mary: Your repeated physical and verbal abuse cannot be justified under any circumstances. Your enabling actions to facilitate the sexual abuse are inexcusable. I cannot imagine what drove you both to the depths of these twisted and inhumane actions. Any justification you give could never be adequate for the damage you have done. You got away with the abuse in our physical world, but you are paying the penance in the spiritual world.

Thank you both for making me who I am today. It is because of you that I have the driving tenacity to succeed at anything in life. Ray, I am far stronger physically and spiritually that you could ever imagine. Mary, I surpass you in every aspect of humanity. I have broken the cycle and share peace with all those I interact with. Ray and Mary don't come around anymore trying to communicate. All I have to say is FUCK YOU! I let go of the hate so I can heal. I broke the cycle. You will never hurt me again. FUCK YOU! I WON

EPILOGUE

I am not sure if this book has an ending. I feel as if it will remain a work in progress so long as the lost souls can glean some inspiration to change their situation. When I first started writing this book, I had only talked about my childhood abuse to a few people I am closest to...my wife, my sister, a few others. As I recorded this journey on paper over several years, I started to open up to others about my experiences. And so many of them—too many of them—have their own stories of abuse. By ridding myself of the shame and claiming my narrative, I am helping them do the same. I am humbled by this. And I am blessed to be constantly reminded of my impact on others and how they find inspiration from my victory over life challenges.

As I reflect on all the adversity I have faced and overcome in my life, I cannot imagine just sitting back and watching the grass grow. I am certain there will be more challenges thrown in my path. I am confident I will face them just as I have with every other difficulty in life—head on with tenacity. I don't idle well. I have no doubt there is some new endeavor I will surge headlong into with all the passion that I bring to those before.

People always ask me "What now? What will you do to replace racing?" Honestly, I am not sure. Not sure I can "replace racing." Life has taught me not to search for the next big thing. Just flow with the rhythm of life. I will find something that fuels my passion.

Until those events occur, I will relish each day that I have been given and be grateful for the opportunity to participate in this wonderful event called "life."

It never gets easy; you just get stronger.

ACKNOWLEDGEMENTS

My wife Marsha, for always loving me unconditionally even when I didn't love myself.

Beth (Wesolowski) Campbell, for without your hard work, attention to detail, and tenacity I could not have achieved the success to put this book to print. I am eternally grateful.

Coach Paul for being there even when you didn't know you were.

My teammates...for a good wheel, a good laugh, a good ass kicking, and a good time.

Tom F., for giving me the tools to set me free.

My family, for their unwavering support in all endeavors and for tolerating all my imperfections, and for standing beside me as I traveled this bumpy road called life.

A higher power for guiding me when I was lost.

My sister, for her unconditional love and support in my darkest hour.

My ESF family, for supporting me as I faced my demons and beat my addiction.

Lee D., for always being there and always raising the bar. You will always be my toughest competition and best pit man.

Curt J., the best lead out man a sprinter could ever hope for. Thank you for listening and never judging.

Dave R., for bestowing upon me life lessons of respect and honor.

Dr. Bill M., for putting Humpty Dumpty back together again. Your patience and precision of reconstructing my teeth to the highest level of aesthetic beauty and functionality is truly a work of art.

Tom and Joann R., for giving me a safe haven even when you didn't realize I needed one.

Mike R. and Peter C. at WB, for keeping my race gear in top condition and caring more about me as a person than the bottom line on the balance sheet.

Paul B., for understanding.

Chris N., for showing me the path to enlightenment.

Tim L. for listening.

Chiseled Chuck for showing me the way; encouraging me; believing in me; and never judging me.

All the Elite Athletes I have been blessed to train with and race against over the decades. You know who you are.

ABOUT THE AUTHOR

Mike Wesolowski is now living his best life of sobriety and inner peace in the Pacific Northwest with his wife Marsha, their adult children, and grandchildren.

When his duties as patriarch of his family, successful businessman, coach, mentor, and athlete are complete, Mike can usually be found on his bike. He rides more miles than he drives each year.

Mike is grateful for each day that he can participate in this wonderful event called "LIFE."

www.ingramcontent.com/pod-product-compliance
Lightning Source LLC
Chambersburg PA
CBHW052013150726
47999CB00004B/1636